Werewolves

A Thematic Analysis of Recent Depictions

(The Truth Behind History's Scariest Shape Shifters)

Robert Davis

Published By **Chris David**

Robert Davis

Werewolves: A Thematic Analysis of Recent Depictions (The Truth Behind History's Scariest Shape Shifters)

ISBN   978-1-77485-718-2

Legal & Disclaimer

The information contained in this ebook is not designed to replace or take the place of any form of medicine or professional medical advice. The information in this ebook has been provided for educational & entertainment purposes only.

The information contained in this book has been compiled from sources deemed reliable, and it is accurate to the best of the Author's knowledge; however, the Author cannot guarantee its accuracy and validity and cannot be held liable for any errors or omissions. Changes are periodically made to this book. You must consult your doctor or get professional medical advice before using any of the suggested remedies, techniques, or information in this book.

Upon using the information contained in this book, you agree to hold harmless the Author from and against any damages, costs, and expenses, including any legal fees potentially resulting from the application of any of the

TABLE OF CONTENTS

Introduction

A werewolf can be described as a mysterious and mysterious beast. The folklore of all around globe recounts tales of gigantic wild wolves who hunt the countryside to catch prey, and terrorizing and killing victims. These stories have been a source of inspiration to the popular fiction writers who have built their work on the myth, giving new rules and depths to this old creature. In the medieval literature there are many tales of villages that were ripped apart by werewolves who have uncontrollable bloodlust, and a constant craving to eat human flesh. In the daytime however, these beasts are not visible. The only proof of their existence is the finding of dead bodies that appear to have been broken by something that has claws and bloody footprints on the paws marking the last steps of the killer.

AFFECTING HUMAN MEAT

Oft, the person who was behind the werewolf was responsible for such horrific actions of violence that were so vile to people that they were deemed by some to have been working with Satan himself. The cannibal killer has the same craving for blood and meat like the midnight predator and the werewolf. It's not surprising that murderers were referred to as werewolves and were often executed in a very brutal manner. Certain people believed in the legend of the werewolf. Wolf hunts were a common practice and were killed because of the fear of metamorphosing into a more dangersome beast in the night.

In the day, identifying an alleged werewolf was simply a matter of seeking out clues. Eyebrows that converged across your bridge noses were usually suspected, as were people with hair on their legs. This was a condition that was that was difficult to prove until the suspect died unfortunately. In the werewolf frenzies that occurred in the middle ages of Europe the people learned to stay away from areas where creatures were believed to gather. It was a good idea to be cautious about becoming a werewolf yourself; people were warned not drink water from "enchanted streams, or to accept strange salve or ointments from strangers. Seventh children born into a family was usually be killed in the first few days of birth or abandoned, in the belief that in the future it would answer the calls from the wild.

Wearing a belt made of wolfskin was believed by some to transform you into a werewolf, just as was wearing a lycanthropic lily and eating the flesh of victim. There was plenty to be remembered in these mysterious and spooky times.

Man's Alter EGO

As time went by and advancements in the field of psychology and medicine were developed, mental illness quickly was blamed as the result of man's alter ego popping out of the shadows uninvited. A werewolf is obviously, a great illustration of the 'duality man'. There is a wild, raw force within us all and when we're beaten and we feel the desire to defend ourselves. The anger may escalate until it is able to be contained not anymore. Most of us, we are able to control this beast using rational thinking. For some, it's difficult to stop and when the monster within is in control, the consequences could be catastrophic. Andrei Chikatilo, the notorious Russian serial killer, was so enthralled by his desire to be the best that he literally ate the flesh of the victims. A person who behaves this way is completely alien to societyand it's simple to understand why this wild behavior was blamed on supernatural forces in the in the past. It was perhaps easier than acknowledging that humans have the capacity to cut each apart and devour the body parts exposed.

The origins of the genre are in folklore and the werewolf is a part of the horror pantheon that is becoming more and more well-known. They are the most savage creature, along with the recently romanticized vampire as well as the somewhat humorous zombie. The werewolf is a runner which gives it an immediate edge over the supernatural counterparts as well as the advantage of enjoying the daylight hours, something that other creatures are unable to enjoy on unless you're the very attractive Edward Cullen, that is. The red blood that runs through the veins of a werewolf with the primal instincts that make them more an equal opponent to vampires or zombie.

Through folklore that inspired stories that are popular, the myth of the werewolf is portrayed in film, literature TV, music and literature. Scottish novelist Robert Louis Stevenson wrote The Strange Case of Dr Jekyll and Mr Hyde in 1886. The story is about one man who has a dual self, with a double mind and an allegory for the good and evil in every person. Jekyll refers to his evil counterpart Mr Hyde as 'the animal within me' as well as the 'caged creature that can't be ignored'. The story might not be a true werewolf tale however it is the model for all of the transformation and werewolf stories that came after. Similar to the way Frankenstein was the catalyst for the reanimation of the zombie and Dracula created vampires, Jekyll and Hyde taught the reader about the 'wolf in us which was revealed through drinking an intoxicant. Another method of transformation in the realm of werewolves can occur by a magical amulet an hex or curse, or even through genetics that are bad. Scott Howard, in Teen Wolf is transformed into a werewolf when puberty kicks into play, a theme that is also featured for the first time in Ginger Snaps, albeit tackled entirely differently. The most well-known werewolf-themed films The Wolf Man, from 1941's The Wolf Man, introduced us to Larry Talbot (played by Lon Chaney Jr.) and the werewolf laws we're now well-known. The film taught us that the transformation between man and werewolf happens in the light from the night sky. Also, it taught us that the use of silver (a bullet, or just an object) will be your most powerful weapon in the fight against Wolfman.

Remorse and regret

The human version of a werewolf, as depicted in the world of fiction, is usually a good character during the daylight. After a wild night out the werewolf is able to wake up with a face that is human filled with regret. The werewolves from Being Human and Buffy the Vampire Slayer are so worried about their condition that they begin locking themselves inside when they are aware that they are about to undergo a transformation. Remus Lupin in Harry Potter and the Prisoner of Azkaban is so disturbed by his condition that he consumes every day a Wolfsbane potion to manage his inner beast. The werewolves in Stephenie Meyer's Twilight series possess a more savage nature, and are 'phase' in the event that they have to defend themselves as well as defend themselves. The portrayal in the character of Jacob Black in his werewolf state is more cuddly than those from Dog Soldiers. The werewolf battles against the two aspects of his personality. In the daytime the human-wolf is embarrassed of its gruesome nighttime activities, but when it's dark their conscience as a werewolf is crystal unmistakable and they have no hesitation in ripping off innocent flesh.

The 16th century physician, botanistand alchemist, astrologer, as well as the occultist Paracelsus believed that each person is a combination of two spirits: the animal spirit as well as the human spirit. The stronger side of a person's personality determines their soul when they die. The human desire for food and pleasure on earth will cause to the ghost of the afterlife to wander throughout eternity in the form of an animal of the wild, such as an wolf, unleashing destruction and revenge on human beings on earth.

Silver BULLETS

It's no wonder that our culture and imagination is so brimming with myths and images of lupines. Recent studies have revealed how organized and hierarchical society of the wolf is. Both wolves and humans have many things in similarities. Man is part of family known as the family just like the wolf and is one of the greatest survivors of evolution. The wolf may be considered to have been the main opponent of mankind in the battle for supremacy. Through time, we have been fighting over the same food source, particularly when it was scarce availability. It was either kill or die. An unarmed man cannot stand up to the wolf. However, humans invented guns. In the past it was bows and spears but nowadays, it's guns. Be sure to load those silver bullets however to ensure.

Chapter 1: Where All Got Started

When I first started going to school I was taught that "civilisation" was not spread to much prior to when Christ was born. Christ. Perhaps maybe a couple hundred years. Prior to this, it was doing nothing but slapping one another over the head with heavy objects.

It's likely due to the fact that our educators were part of the generation of Mortimer Wheeler and had been educated classically. They believed that the Romans brought us civilization and were good.

The Romans weren't the ones to bring us civilization, but they introduced us to writing.

They were far from innocent. You can read their comments on the sucking of Celtic tribes into the Empire!

There was a very successful civilisation prior to that. We had history, religion and medicine, engineering, agricultural efficiency, astronomy as well as a well-established international trade system and a high-quality level of culture. It would have been impossible to have constructed Stonehenge with out it. It's just mostly oral. (That is the reason according to Pliny the Elder Pliny the Elder, the Druids were awed by memory over all things).

It was also many thousands of years earlier than Rome.

In the beginning of high school, students were taught that it was difficult to think of a duration as long as two thousand years. That's partially correct but the whole foundation of our modern civilisation was laid down thousands of years ago before Christ.

The first 18 years that followed have been spent learning the things we knew from the Bronze Age and there's not an archaeologist or a serious historian anywhere on earth who's not convinced.

the Minoans in Thera (Santorini) were an extensive trading empire that covered the globe. There is strong evidence that they extracted a significant amount of the copper that fueled the Bronze Age from North America.

The early Greeks (around 500 BCE) had an initial steam-engine prototype, automated vending machines that operated on coins in their temples, fully automated three-act theatre shows and portable analogue astronomical computer systems that we're incredibly pushed to replicate in the present. They even developed railways.

Unexpectedly, around the year 1206 BCE, Bronze Age high-civilisation was largely ended. There are evidences of a devastating droughts, widespread, and other things.

After that followed the Romans. Militaristic and an unworthy excuse for a civilisation which was followed immediately by the Church of Rome, whose stupid, power-mad, totalitarian regime ruled over the most dark period of human history, and led to the dismantling of culture and science. Aristarchus from Samos was wiped out of history, Giordano Bruno was burned alive, Galileo Galilei was brutally placed under house arrest during the last 10 years of his life in addition to Isaac Newton came perilously close to being tried for heresy and was burnt to death for working out a tiny calculation:

However, enough with the tiny things. Imagine two millennia of time.

Imagine four thousand.

Try to get your head around the timescale. Please note to note that these times are approximate because they are based on geographical locations.

The age of enlightenment from 1650's up to 1780's

Renaissance The period from 1350's to 1650's

The Middle Ages (Medieval) 5th-15th centuries

The Dark Ages, 4th through 8th century

Roman Period: 600 BCE to 400 AD

Iron Age: 1,200 BCE to 600 AD

Bronze Age: 3,300 BCE to 1,200 BCE

Neolithic from 10,000 BC to 3300 BCE

Mesolithic from between 20,000 BCE up to 10,000 BCE

Upper Paleolithic: 50,000 BCE to 20,000 BCE

The rest of Paleolithic: 2.6 million years between 50,000 and 2.6 million years ago.

You can't, right?

Also, you shouldn't be capable of.

What does this mean?

It's a sign hominins (human predecessors) have existed over 2.6 millions of years. I'm giving this information only to help you understand but it's not crucial in this book.

MODERN Humans (that is the homo sapiens) have been around for over 200,000 years.

By "modern humans" I'm talking about US. Not just a little bit like us but thick and hairy.

You can think of people that you could place in modern society that could perform as well as, or even better than you or me. Same exact body. Same exact brain. Just as intelligent and sophisticated as I am (just not as classy).

In the vast majority of the time, we've been on the same planet as different species of human (or hominins) which includes homo Erectus and the homo neanderthalensis (Neanderthals) as well as the homofloresiensis ("the hobbit") and the Denisovans of whom no one knows very much.

Neanderthals went extinct 36,000 years ago, and no one is sure why. Theories of competition are most likely but one of the shockingly not-known facts about Neanderthals was that they had bigger brain capacity than us. This means that they had larger brains. So , what were they using all that brain power? We do not know.

There's another surprise - we crossed with them. It's true to a large extent. We now share 2percent in all of the Neanderthal genome!

As I mentioned that, this is all to help you get started.

Who can tell what someone as intelligent and sophisticated as we were doing, thinking, and worshipping around 200,000 years back?

We have a pretty clear idea of about what they were doing and thinking about 40 years ago. We also know at a minimum, what their spiritual or religious practices were.

How?

Cave art is everywhere - plenty of it.

Artifacts - a lot of them.

A detailed analysis of the present-day indigenous peoples across the globe and who live EXACTLY exactly the same as. They include a variety of African tribes, including those of the Bushmen from the Kalahari (who are the most valuable and dangerously endangered human connection to the hunter-gatherers of early homo sapiens) as well as people from the Aboriginal tribes from Australia as well as the nomadic peoples from Siberia, Finland and Lapland and the traditional Native Americans.

Before this becomes an explanation of archaeology (or the study of anthropology) I'll explain what I mean by archaeology.

Here are some contemporary art works of shamanic that are from North America, Africa and Australia :

It's true that some images resemble Salvador Dali is getting down, however the stunning rendition of the animals is apparent throughout the collection as are images that depict half-humans or half-animals.

We refer to this as THERIANTHROPY also known as THERIOCEPHALY and, when referring to modern-day First Nation shamans, it typically describes the shaman's journey into"the "spirit realm" to establish the "blueprint" for the upcoming hunt or activity. The shaman assumes the traits of a particular animal in order to increase their powers and to be able to communicate with the animals or their species, or to make a symbolic sacrifice, and "prefigure" the hunt that is to be planned by playing the role of the prey animal, and then being killed in the spirit realm.

I stated "most frequently". Because sometimes , the shaman believes that he or she could become the animal physically.

However, more often than not it is the tribe or people of the shaman that believe in this. The ignorant and foolish hoi polloi.

I use this expression lightly in a humorous way since there is a fervent traditional component in all contemporary shamanic groups who firmly and firmly are believers in the notion of what Native American peoples call SKINWALKERS.

Skinwalkers are individuals who, for any reason, are able to transform physically into animals. Sometimes, just one, and at times, any animal wants to. The pelt of the animal has to be worn, but this isn't an unwritten rule. In fact today it's just a little bit of a gift.

They usually are sorcerers or witches wicked people who are against the natural laws. However, there are exceptions.

Before we get into more details about skinwalkers, have the following look:

I'll go over some of them individually in the future however these are not contemporary shamanic cave art from North America, Africa or Australia. They're between 15,000 and 40000 years old, and are originated from the western part of Europe!

Pay attention to the animals. Da Vinci may have sketched them. Notice the ubiquitous images of monster-men. Therianthropes.

In terms of who created these beautiful and horrifying images is concerned The species is the same, the practices are identical, the manner of living is the same, and the BELIEFS are identical. It was us. It was a long, unimaginably long time ago in the haze of the distant past when strange forms walked among real monsters.

Chapter 2: Art Sorcery, Werewolves And

All the way to (and up to and including) all the way to the Iron Age, art, science and medicine, astronomy and mathematics, as well as metallurgy and divination, navigation, and astrology were all part of the same topic. MAGIC.

The art of magic (or magic or) was SECRET knowledge. It was not a state secret, but more of a trade secret, and was consciously kept secret.

The exact parallels can be drawn between modern hunter-gatherer societies , where people who can treat accidents, manage, anticipate the astronomical future and (as as the natural cures will let) treat the sick, hold immense and real power over their groups (not to be left out their status).

A large portion of the Shaman's (that is the magician's) knowledge of astronomy, medicine navigation, navigation, etc. is not awe-inspiring or insignificant, but is based on sound research, evidence-based science and information passed down through oral transmission.

All the things a shaman can do serves a function. There is no place in the primitive world for anything else, and that includes divination, magic or trance states, as well as communicating to the deceased or animal spirits.

Whatever the sorcerer does grants the sorcerer control over their surroundings (and over their own people) and, if there is no codified mathematical system What is the simplest and most straightforward method of expressing and influencing the world?

ART.

Without writing numbers, mathematical symbols or even numbers We represent the things we do, observe and work with, or want to influence by rendering images of them. Drawing them.

It is possible to draw drawings of the results we want to achieve or the changes we wish to bring about in the world that surrounds us.

It is now, certain, MAGIC.

It's a mix of the two: a prayer and a spell. It's possible to combine this with traveling to the spirit realm to effect these changes on the "higher level" this becomes more effective.

There are hundreds of breathtaking cave paintings dating to cave paintings dating back to the Upper Paleolithic and very few of the caves they are displayed were ever used for living. Furthermore, in caves that show evidence of domestic activity paintings are found in the darkest, deepest basement recesses , where there is no evidence of domestic activities.

This kind of art kept from the rest of society, but it's also kept secret. It's a regulated activity that is only undertaken by a select few. Only a select small number of.

They weren't eccentrics or the outcasts of their clans, tribes or tribes They are the Talent. The most thought-provoking thinkers. You can tell that in their artwork.

Consider Leonardo Da Vinci, who was an alchemist of a renowned calibre and Kabbalist along with all the other things we admire his work for.

Isaac Newton was also a important alchemist, with a "Natural philosophy" was strongly linked into Kabbalah. Kabbalah and he devoted the majority of his life engaged in the pursuit of these ideas.

We'll return to the secret art of an omen or prayer. An enchanted equation or algorithm.

If you look at this amazing gorgeous art work - truly look at it - you cannot avoid being awestruck by the talent as well as the talent, moving, the pure vitality of it all. The mind immediately connects to Leonardo Da Vinci and Michelangelo Buonarroti.

You might also be wondering where they did their practice. Although there's an indication of some practice within caves, there is small, if any. It is possible that they did their practice on flat stones near an eddy and allowed the river to wash half-formed art (and the magic).

No matter what I've included, below, a gallery of ten masterworks that belong to the paleolithic. Certain are multiples, which benefit from an angle or light:

Finally, think of Edvard Munsch and the sheer feeling of human movement within "The Scream":

None of them, as breathtakingly beautiful as they may be were created in ars gratia artis (art for the sake of art).

They vary between 41,000 and 41,000 in El Castillo cave, Spain and up to 35,000 years old or older in Lascaux as well as Chauvet caves located in France to numerous other sites however they are ALL amazing contracts.

These and other items that are that are coming out testify to a long-standing society that has an established culture and a refined aesthetic. But more than that they are a testimony to the magical.

What kind of magic could be inferred from the examples that are listed below? They form part aspects of evidence (but only a small portion) for the extrapolations to be dealt in the next chapter.

You might have been completely amazed by the beauty of the two-dimensional artwork of cave walls as shown above (and justly so) aside from the staggering and inconceivable time, but here's a surprise that's sure to make you shiver and will leave you speechless!

This one's located in Montespan, France and is approximately 20,000-25,000 years old.

The next one might also be from the work of a European Master of the Renaissance:

It's true that it's an old-fashioned "reclining naked" However, it's 15,000 year old in La Magdelaine cave , France.

There's many more, but this is the one that really hits you in the face that's sure to get you to sleep. This isn't a thin layer of an ochre-colored wall in a cave. It's a sculpture:

It's not 32,000 older, like one the captions claims. Recent studies have proved that it is 40,000 years old!

Here's the first evidence of shamanic rituals and it's an animal that was once a were-animal. A man sporting a lion's head, an therianthrope.

It was discovered in a cave located in Hohlenstein Stadel, Germany in 1939, but was only rebuilt following the war.

The figure wears an apron and is a male (no bras). The head of the figure is an European cave lion (Panthera Leo Spelaea) Males of this species do not have a mane. It's the same kind of lion that is depicted with multiples within the amazing cave paintings of Chauvet, France, above.

Shamanism is the earliest and the most fundamental form of organized "religious" practice. It was thought previously that the pre-eminent evidence of its existence was located at the Czech Republic and dated around 30000 BCE (excitingly in close proximity the time of Transylvania, Moldova and Carpathia where many of our vampire and werewolf legends began) however, here it is 11,000 years old and located located in Germany.

The earlier paleolithic figurines or carvings were not much more than the blurry "Venus in the town of Willendorf." It is true I am aware the fact that it is an illustration of an abstract, idealized, or divine concept , but I'm mostly concerned with the design, the execution and the method used by the artist. It's about a foot tall and was carved from solid ivory by masters.

A second lion-headed statue that was of the same period was discovered in a cave within the same area (the Swabian Alps) along with a number of bone flutes. One of the flutes was carved from mammoth ivory, and the other was made is made of a bone from one of Griffon Vulture.

Music and animals. Ritual. Ceremony. Shamanism.

This is in perfect harmony with the current knowledge of Shamanic practices.

A 40-year-old flute made of the bones of an Griffon Vulture. It was found alongside a lion-headed human.

Chapter 3: The Link

Are there modern Shamans living in an environment identical to Europe 40000 years ago?

So, what was going on in Europe 40 years ago?

The last ice age started at 100,000 years old and came to an end 11,500 years ago, but it wasn't just all snow and ice.

In the 40,000 years prior to when temperatures were average, it was just five degrees cooler than the current temperature. Things got wild.

There was a complete , rapid change in the geomagnetic field of the Earth that took about 450 years to complete with an average strength of just 25% of current value.

Then the climate became colder and stayed this way until the final Glacial Maximum of 24,000 to 18,000 years ago.

Who lives within the Ice Age?

The nomadic peoples of Siberia and those of the Native American Peoples of Alaska and the Yukon.

Everyone is aware of the Inuit and the Haida and others First Nation peoples of the American and Canadian North West but who has been exposed to much (if any) about the Siberians from the Native Peoples?

The story of Native Siberian Peoples is a tragic one, with their treatment by those who were Russians and, in turn the Soviets was far as shameful and shaming than way of treating Native Americans. As with many of the Native Americans, this shameful treatment continues to be a problem, sub rosa, even today.

One online source provides the most poignant claim that today there are less Native Siberians across the entire of Siberia than Native Americans in the single state of Arizona.

True genocide was the norm here, and for the Aleuts by themselves, all men were slaughtered, and the women and children were sold to slavery.

In the remaining part of Siberia the herds of reindeer of the native tribes were simply confiscated and sold to Russian incomers by the Czars and then the Soviets followed them. The wild game was also confiscated. Herds of reindeer constitute the most important means to survive in this environment and have been neglected until they are at risk of disappearance and the pattern persists.

Languages are classified by their language. There are four distinct groups comprising Native Siberian peoples, the Uralic and the Altaic and the Yeniseian and the Paleosiberian and, though their languages of origin are usually inextricably linked the shamanic practices of their people are generally identical.

It is imperative to recognize that these shamanic practices are at risk of being destroyed following hundreds of years of deliberate attempts to eradicate them by the rabidly Orthodox Christian Czars the despotic, genocidal insane communists. The principal goal here was to simply eliminate the shamans in themselves.

In spite of everything the shamanic practice was so strong in this region that the bulk of it is still alive and has been passed on in oral tradition, just like it has always been. The problem is that there are so few people living there and even less people who are shamans.

Here's the head of a Siberian Shaman who was depicted by the 1790's. Be sure to pay focus to the fascinating head-gear

Have an eye on this:

This is a headdress found in the Star Carr cave dated around 9000 years old. It has three Harpoon points.

It is also an inscription from Star Carr with a 9,900 years.

The rest come of BedburgThe rest are mostly from Bedburg Konigshoven, Germany, dated around 10,000 years ago.

Some of them appear frightening even today.

They are all from different regions of the globe and at different times of the day, but their purpose is exactly identical, as is the shamanic tradition that they are derived.

We are now back back to our Sorcerer inside the caverns of Lascaux.

After a make-over, it appears like this:

Or, this:

Here's the Sorcerer who appears during an ritual, and how he would like to enter the realm of the spirit and possess the characteristics of specific animals with the capability to talk to them.

It is possible to see a part of the deer's skull when it is positioned on top of his owl's face.

This painting was appropriately named "The Sorcerer" by its creators. It's powerful and primordial like these head-strong (or bison-headed) men from the same time period One from Lascaux, and another from Gabilou:

Compare this to Siberian rock art from 3,500 years ago:

and Siberian rock art that was created just about 400 years earlier:

Take note of the headdress.

There are many other similarities between Mesolithic and modern art of shamanism However. Have a look at the following "hunting scene" which is also from Lascaux and 15,000 years old.

It's often described as "The Hunting Accident" however it isn't unintentional.

I will quote Eric Edwards:

"The Shaman needs maximum support from animals on his journey. The shaman wears an owl's eyes, ears of wolves horses tails and bears paws and dances (Lissner 1961). The antlers of deer as well as bear feet have been proven to be most effective magic equipment (Ucko 1967). The "man who is accompanied by a bison' from the Shaft at Lascaux is a shamanic occurrence featuring a sacrificed bison as well as an untidy man (with an animal mask) sitting on the ground in a state of trance (Lissner 1961). The rhinoceros that is in the composition is of no significance because it's the bison and man facing off (Blanc 1949). The supine figure represents the shaman as well as the bird is his spirit of tutelary and its perch is an erect or a sky-pole. The wood bird poles represent the spiritual journey of a shaman, and are "...a way to heaven , symbolized with an upright pole as well as the belief that birds is able to carry a soul of a shaman through the skies." (Lissner 1961). The entire is a multifaceted piece that contains evidence of totemic beliefs and shamanic practice as well as fertility rituals."

I'd suggest that the stick-figure character of the shaman can be seen as a symbol of the spirit world , and contrasts with the intense realistic nature of bison. The man's erection symbolizes an emotional state.

Another time, Eric Edwards said it earlier than me:

"The cave painting in Lascaux, France, circa 15.000 to 10,000 BC. (shown above) This can be explained through Siberian myths from the modern era. A spear appears to have struck the bison, and then eviscerated the animal. The shaman takes his spirit to Heaven when lying in a state of death (Lommel 1966) while he hunts animal spirits or talks with the mistress of the Animals. There are a variety of signs that indicate the shamanic origins of the work. It is gallinaceous, or similar to a grouse carving of a spear-thrower in Le Mas d'Azil (Davenport, 1988). Humanoid feet like the phallus, but the hands are four-toed, like a bird's and thus is a symbol of pictography. The artist has depicted the shaman in the form of his spirit-guide (the bird-eyed wand) in the process of his transformation, or transformation to the form of a Black Grouse or Capercaille (Davenport 1988) This is a show that was common to Palaeolithic hunter, and resembling the dances of the community as well as the strutting and fighting rituals in the Blackcock.

"The key to successful hunting is imitation (Lommel 1966) The successful hunt is imagined by the shaman prior to the hunt. The bison's entrails are snared out with barbed spears and the entire image explains that to Abbre Breuil (1965) that the hunter gets wounded by bison, and later is killed by the rhinoceros in contrast, for Leroi Gourhan the hunter suffers from the wounds caused by bison (Lissner 1961). However, the shaman appears probably in the state of trance. The rock art of South Africa is historical evidence for the role of ceremonies and hallucinogens as well as trance. maybe "...decorated caves found in Palaeolithic Europe during the close of the Ice Age, might also be a reflection of shamanic practices and rituals of trance." (Pitts 2001).

"In the shamanistic tradition, were commonplace in the early Celtic divinations, they carried cloaks made from birds' feathers similar to what the Siberians were doing, keeping on that Celtic faith in metamorphosis, the ability to change shape - or alter appearance or form at any time. In Santander you can see wall paintings of people wearing bird masks, who appear to be dancing. the bird-men from Altamira can also be shamans similar to the masked figure in Les Combarelles (Lissner, 1961). In Teyat, Abri Mege (Dordogne) three bizarre figures that resemble sea horses are likely Shamans wearing Ibex masks. There are other examples of hybrid characters that are hunters and shamans that occupy territories between the animal and human worlds (Grazioli 1960). There is also evidence that shamans used birds as tutelary spirits , or spirit guides for rituals involving shamanism (Davenport 1988) For instance, the Lascaux'man with bison'.

"Palaeolithic batons, also known as "wands" could be shamans drumsticks, but certainly more than objects of daily use (Lissner 1961) female statuettes are among the first recognized figurative representations of women around the globe and could play a role in shamanic rituals as dolls used for auxiliary purposes. Female statuettes from Siberian tribes, which frequently had female shamans or'shamankas were likely to have had an important role in ritual. In Ma'lta 50 miles to the north of Irkutsk female figures as well as birds made of bone depict ducks and geese. They are similar to bird-like figures that contemporary Siberian tribes put on the top of their sacred sky-poles.In regard to how shamanic mobility art might not have been long-lasting - such as sky-poles, wands drums, as well as other tools like masks - it's possible that engravings made on portable devices of birds could have played an shamanic ritual and role."

Have a look the Native American shamanic rock art images and tell me if you can't see striking resemblances to the bird-headed man in the movie and "bird-on-a-stick" within"Hunting Accident. "Hunting accident".

In addition to the content, but also how it is executed, composed and the technique.

Shapeshifters are found in stories of ALL people, but nowhere are they more popular as in folklore from those of Celtic, Gaulish, Slavic and Teutonic peoples of Europe (not even in Africa). The werewolf is a unique European myth, despite the jackal-headed god , Anubis, of the past of Egypt as well as other gods and gods. The shapeshifter as well as the skinwalker are popular within Native American lore, the werewolf is an exotic species.

It was a result of the Celtic dark twilight of Europe.

THE END

This is the end of Book One.

I truly hope that you enjoyed the book. It's the bulk of the ancient history rewritten. However, I won't allow you to go, without releasing you ....

A TEST BOOK TWO TASTER!

In which you can find a wealth of thoroughly researched REPORTS, ACCOUNTS and SIGHTINGS of WEREWOLVES up to today.

ACCOUNTS LIKE THIS ....

"Between 1526-1630, there were about 30,000 written and recorded stories of werewolves from Central France alone! There are many more reports from Germany, Russia, Hungary, Spain, Holland, Belgium, Norway, Denmark, Sweden, Iceland, Lapland, Finland and the UK."

OR OR THIS ....

The Werewolf of Dole.

Gilles Garnier was a reclusive hermit who lived outside of Dole, a town in Dole in Franche-Comte France. He was recently married and relocated his new wife to his isolated home. Not used of feeding more himself , he had difficulty to feed his wife which caused unrest between the two. At this time many children disappeared or were discovered dead and half-eaten, and the provincial authorities issued an order encouraging and allowing citizens to hunt down and kill the responsible werewolf. In the evening, a group of people traveling from a nearby town were able to spot what they believed in the dark as a wild animal, but it was regarded by some as a hermit who was surrounded by the corpse of a deceased child. The next day, Gilles Garnier was arrested. Many people who were his victimized between nine and twelve-year-olds. Garnier typically ate flesh of their legs, thighs and bellies, which is a common trait in some kind of "werewolf" which will be seen time and time again.

Garnier's confession entailed an "spectre" that appeared before him at night and handed him an ointment bottle that enabled him to transform into the Wolf.

As with all werewolves, he was questioned by secular authorities and was being found guilty of witchcraft as well as lycanthropy . He was then burned alive, in the stake.

OR OR THIS ....

On the 31st of October 1999. A young lady named Doristine Gipson, from nearby Elkhorn was driving along Bray Road near Delavan. As she approached the intersection with Hospital Road, she leaned over to switch the radio station when she noticed the front tire of her right side leap off the ground like she hit something. Bewildered, she stopped her vehicle and went out to find out what had happened. Not finding anything in front of her car and she started looking at the surroundings. When she looked into the dark she was able to see a hairy, dark figure speeding towards her. She was unable to see the form from the distance she was (about fifty feet) however, she could see that the person was large and later would compare the figure to someone who exercises continuously using weights. Incredulous at the appearance of the figure and by the sound that it made of "heavy feet" and "heavy feet," she swiftly retreated to her vehicle. She jumped into her car and attempted to leave when the beast leapt into her car. Luckily it was too wet for the beast to stay on and dropped to the ground. Doristine went back to the spot later in the evening with a child was out for trick-or-treating, and saw a huge creature on the other roadway's side. When she saw the beast moving, she instructed the child to secure her door , and quickly drove to get away.

Chapter 4: The Myth Of The Werewolf

SUPERHUMAN STRENGTH

They are usually described as having incredible strength and enhanced senses that are far more powerful than wolves, and definitely more powerful than humans. They possess all the characteristics of a wolf , including powerful jaws, powerful teeth, and larger paws capable of doing a good amount of damage to any creature. In some tales they are also said to have killed using knives or daggers.

In their unaltered, human form, werewolves are said to show obvious evidence of their altered appearance. For instance, the eyebrows that of a person who transforms into a waswolf are usually believed to meet on the bridge of the nose. They are characterized by curved fingernails and ears that sit low on the top of the head, and they walk in a loping, swinging stride. They are believed to be dull, deficient in energy, and eager to stay away from exposure to sunlight. Also, they find cooking food repellent. There is a popular belief that the only body part that isn't changed when the human body transforms into a werewolf is the eyes. They remain human even though they could, if the creature is furious appear to be burning. They also are unable to shed tears. Werewolves are, as you might expect, unable to cry.

It is believed it is believed that when you slice into the meat of a waswolf when it is in human form, under the flesh you will be able to see its fur. The Russians are, however, of the opinion that one can establish to be a waswolf by the bristles on his tongue. What they look like differs depending on the culture they are in but they are typically depicted as lacking tails, similar to their supernatural counterparts, witches do not possess tails when taking forms of animal.

In the area of Scandinavia called Fennoscandia the werewolves were typically elderly women who had claws that were encased with poison. They had the capability of causing paralysis to animals and children by their eyes. While in Serbia the vampires (used as a reference in Serbian folklore to describe vampires and werewolves) are believed to come in winter to reunite. They would remove their wolfskins, and hang them on trees. When they got together they would grab one animal skin and throw it into the fire, freeing the owner of the curse that turned it into a werewolf or vampire.

In Haiti there are werewolves called je-rouges that try to take children away from their mothers at evening, by waking them up even while they're asleep and asking permission to steal their child. Mothers who are confused may decide to say yes, and regret it for the rest of their lives.

From WEREWOLF to HUMAN

Returning to human form can be a terrifying moment for the werewolf. The werewolf is frequently seen to be weak and fragile and likely to be depressed to the point of being severely depressed. The scale of crimes that were committed as a animal renders the werewolf regretful and suffering from melancholia as well as horrible guilt. among the many horrific crimes that were that were committed during the medieval period of Europe was the horrific habit of eating dead corpses.

The process of becoming a Werewolf

Folklore and legends provide the many ways to transform into werewolves. The most straightforward and, possibly, the most well-known in the history of legends is to take off any clothing and put on an elkskin-covered belt or, in some cases human skin that has been removed out of the body of a criminal who has been executed. A girdle, also known as a belt in some cases should be at least three fingers large.

Movies illustrate that another method to attain the power to transform into a werewolf is to get bitten by a werewolf. This results in the saliva of the animal entering the bloodstream, triggering the power. However, this method is a source of ridicule for those who believe that when someone is bit by a werewolf and is bitten, the victim seldom survives the experience and therefore would not be alive enough to transform into a werewolf.

FULL MOON

It was believed that, in Italy, France and Germany there was a legend that a person could transform into a werewolf if lay outside on a particular Thursday or Friday night in summer when the full moon was shining directly onto his face.

Drinking water that is derived from those tracks left by wolves can be suggested for those who want to be a werewolf or drinking from specific streams that seem to be enchanted or are where the wolves drink. Consuming the flesh - particularly the heart of a wolf, or anything else killed by a wolf considered to be another method to be a werewolf. In actual fact, Egbert, Archbishop of York who was killed in 766, declared that the meat of animals who had been murdered and slain by wolves shouldn't be consumed to protect against those who ate the flesh becoming werewolves.

However, some sources claim it is believed that eating the dead wolf its victim will have negative effects, in that it actually helps those who consume the flesh of the wolf against a variety of magical magickal enchantments. Human flesh consumption is an opportunity to become werewolves, specifically the flesh of criminals who commit violent crimes.

TRANSFERRED WATERS

Elliot O'Donnell, in his classic work on the topic of Werewolves The Book of Werewolves, provides specifics about how to become werewolves to be a werewolf in Sweden as well as Norway.

The author writes that the person requesting the help must locate a stream that is lycanthropous. Lycanthropous water is different from normal water, and it requires a trained eye to detect it. It has a faint smell like no other and is a "lurid" sparkle to it , which appears to suggest that it has an internal life. The sound it produces is like the sound, or at the very least, mutterings and whispers that humans make. In the night, frightening screaming and groans emanate from it. Animals avoid it , and if they are brought close to it, cower or cry in terror.

While kneeling along the bank of the river The person should be chanting the following words:

Tis the night! etis night! The moon shines white

Over the pine-covered hill and the snow-capped mountain;

The shadows drift through the burn and brae

and dance to that sparkling dance.

It's night! etis night! and the devil's light

The beams cast glimmering light around.

The maras dance, nuss prance

On the ground that is adorned with flowers.

Tis the night! etis night! and the werwolfis may

It makes nature and man shiver.

However, its grey and savage head and sly tread

Do you have anything to offer O river!

River, river, river.

Oh, the water is strong, it flows along,

I'm looking for a Wolf to create me.

All things that are dear to my heart I swear

In death , we will not leave you.

Then, he should strike the bank of the stream three times on the forehead, then dip his head into the water three times, each time taking one mouthful of the enchanted water. After that, he or became an internal werewolf and, within 24 hours the first metamorphosis of the werewolf will begin.

LYCANTHROPOUS FLOWERS

To transform into a werewolf Swedish and Norwegian the supplicants can also pull the lycanthropous flower, and wear it in the evening on a night when moon is at its full. Lycanthropous flower, as with the water of lycanthropous, have characteristics unique to these flowers. The scent of these flowers is believed to be that of death, and their sap is white and sticky even though they look similar to other flowers, usually either yellow or white.

The lycanthropous plant is seen in many different cultures. There is a tale of the Kloska family, who resided in the town of Kerovitch located on the Romanian side of the Transylvanian Alps. Ivan Kloska and Olga Kloska were the children of an owner of a store. One day, leaving with their mother, who was washing clothes in the stream in front of their home The two children walked away. They began to collect flowers however, suddenly Ivan was woken by a loud shout. When he turned around, he saw that his sister was sucked into a pit, which was covered by brambles and weeds. He went down to ensure she wasn't injured. The girl was safe however she told him about an unusual flower that was growing there. It was a bright white flowerthat looked like a sunflower, but it was soft and pulpy. It also released an unpleasant, sweet smell. Olga declared that she was going dress in it however Ivan was concerned because it was something more like a mold rather than flowers and advised her to stay clear of it. As she began crying she cried, but Ivan agreed and let her to attach it to her dress. She wanted to know if the dress looked nice but he then was scared when he stared at her face that changed into what appeared to be, an Wolf!

SURVIVING A WEREWOLF

Certain flowers, like the lily of the valley marigolds and azaleas have been said to draw werewolves, and diamonds are thought to possess the same effect. In the southern part of France as well as in other countries when the moon's full is that a loup-garou transforms from being a wolf to a human regardless of whether it happens by choice or not. The way they usually perform the change is by jumping into the water or fountain, and then emerging with hair and savaged in their way. In order to return to their human appearance, they leap back into the same pool or fountain.

Anglo-Dutch antiquarian Richard Verstegan, wrote in the Restitution of Decayed Intelligence in 1628:

The werewolves are acerbayne sorcerers who after anointing them with an ointment that they create by the inclination of devils and put on a girdle that is a certayne inchaunt they do not at all in the opinions of others appear as wolves, but in their own minds, they have the appearance and the nature of wolves, as long as they wear the girdle. And they behave as wolves in killing and hunting as well as most humane creatures.

A DEADLY FLOWER

Ivan attempted to climb from the pit to warn the mother of his son, but an fight ensued. Their mother, when she heard the sound of fighting, rushed to the scene to find Ivan lying on the ground, trying to ward off the grey wolf who was already biting him and is now trying to come close enough to smack its fangs of yellow through his throat. He yelled to his wife that the Wolf was Olga and explained the flower while the wolf charged at him. The mother of the children had in her possession a skewer she used to attach the washing line of her house to trees but she also faced the dilemma of. If she killed the wolf, she could lose her daughter. If she didn't kill the wolf then she could be losing her son. She made her choice and then threw the skewer into the eye of the wolf. A few hours later the villager, returning home noticed strange noises of laughter. He ran to the side of the pit and lean over. 'Vera Kloska! What are you doing there?', the man shouted. 'Ha! ha! ha!' was the reply. 'My children! Do they not look funny? Olga has a gorgeous buttonhole with a white flower as well as Ivan has a red stain across his forehead. They're deaf. They aren't able to respond when I talk to them. Check if you can get them to hear. The villager shakes his head. They'll never be able to hear again in the world, poor woman", he said. You've killed them.'

Old RUSSIAN SPELL TO REFORMING TO WEREWOLF

To turn into a werewolf enter a forest and locate the tree that was cut down. Place a small, copper-colored knife into it and then walk in circles around the tree, reciting the following:

In the vast, expansive ocean in the small island Bujan

On the plains, the Moon shines brightly on an aspen stump

In the woods of green and into the dark vale

To the left of the herd scurries the shaggy animal

His fangs were sharpened to the cattle with horns

However, into the woods the wolf doesn't go.

He does not dive into the vale of shadows.

Moon, moon! Golden horned moon!

Burn the bullet, then reduce the sharpness of the hunter's knife.

Splinter , the shepherdis' staff

Make terror abound over all cattle

On men and all creepy things

They may not be able to capture the gray the wolf

They should not tear his soft hide!

The word I use is bound, more firm than sleep

More powerful than the promises of heroes!

After that, jump across the trees three times, and you'll have transformed into a werewolf.

Based on Elliott O'Donnell there are a range of methods to turn into werewolves. In some instances it's genetic and runs within the family and there's no way to alter it, even if the gene passes on to them. In other instances it's acquired through rituals that involve black magic that differ based on the locale. There is one thing that is certain however, as per O'Donnell, any person who wishes to become a werewolf should be 100% convinced of the supernatural forces that give the ability.

Anyone who wants to change into a werewolf should find a place that is isolated, away from the crowds. The most suitable locations are wilderness, forests that are remote, or mountains.

THE WITCHING HOURS

The timing is, naturally essential. It's no surprise that the night of your choice must be selected at a time when the moon appears either new or full, as at this time, the influence of the planets are the most favorable. A flat and perfectly flat piece of ground ought to be chosen , and at midnight an area of not less than 7 feet in diameter should be drawn with chalkor when that's not possible use string. Within this, starting from the same point in the centre, is smaller circles, each with a radius of three feet. In the middle of the circles, a fire is required to be lit. Over the fire, constructed an iron tripod on where you can hang an iron water container. As soon as the water starts to boil, a handful of three of the following are to be thrown into the water: asafoetida (a plant that is also known as devil's dung) parsley, opium, hemlock aloe, saffron, henbane poppy-seed or solanum. When they are put into the vessel, following mantra should be repeated:

Spirits from the depth

Who never sleeps

Please be nice to me.

Ghosts of the dead

There is no soul to save

Please be gentle with me.

Tree spirits

It will continue to grow as the leas,

Please be gentle with me

Spirits from the air

Black and black and not fair.

Please be nice to me.

The water spirit is a scourge,

For bathers and ships that are crucial,

Please be gentle with me.

Spirits of earthbound dead

The smooth glide of a silent tread,

Please be nice to me.

Spirits of fire and heat,

Disruptive to your ire.

Please be gentle with me.

Spirits of ice and cold

Criminals as patrons and vice

Please be nice to me.

Wolves, vampires, satyrs, ghost!

Elect among the evil hosts!

I ask you to send me a message,

Hither send it, hither

The fantastic grey shape that makes men sweat!

Shiver, shiver, shiver!

Come! Come! Come!

Anyone who wants to attain these powers must remove his clothes and smear their body in the oil of a dead creature (a cat is the best) that has aniseed and camphor as well. In the abdomen, a girdle or belt made from animal skin must be secured. The supplicant must then sit in the middle of the circle, and wait for the arrival of "the Unknown'. It will be evident that the Unknown will appear when the flame burns blue.

The ARRIVAL OF THE SPIRIT

The great spirit could appear in many ways. There might be an unusually quiet silence prior to the event, but it could also be an abundance of sound including screams, crashes or screaming. It is possible that he will not appear however his presence will be felt by a strange temperature in the air, and the supplicant is overwhelmed with fear. He can appear as the huntsman - the most popular form of him or take the appearance of a monster, part man and part beast. At times, he can appear as if he is hazy, and only appear in a partial way.

O'Donnell affirms that this force does not appear to be devilish but definitely a vengeful, supernatural power , which he says may have been involved in the formation of the Earth as well as the other planets. There are other strategies that can be used to transform into werewolves without having to undergo an experience that is terrifying. The author suggests eating the brains and intestines of an wolf or drinking water derived from the footprints of a werewolf, or even drinking water from a river from where there are three or more werewolves who have been observed to drink.

THE EIGI EINHAMMR

Then, in Norway and Iceland There were people who were called eigi einhammr which means "not of one skin". They were thought have the ability to assume different body types as well as the characteristics of the creatures whose bodies they adopted.

Through it, an einhammr was able to attain extraordinary powers. his strength increased several times over as he maintained his own strength, but also incorporated the power of the creature whose form he was taking. The person who was transformed thus became identified as the hamrammr.

There were many methods of achieving the needed transformation. Sometimes, a pelt would be put over the body and the transformation took place instantly. Other times souls left its human form and went into the corpse of the animal to be submerged. It was then left in a cataleptic state appearing dead to the uninitiated. Another method to trigger the alteration was through incantation. This technique allowed the human form to remain unchanged but the eyes of the observers were enticed, so they could only see him in his altered appearance.

The eigi einhammr in his most pristine form, is visible only through his eyes. They cannot be changed. His behavior, however, remains similar to the creature who has taken his form but his human-like intelligence and wit will be with him. So, he will be able to perform the same things that animals do, while still having the capability to perform what a human being is able to accomplish.

The power of WOLFSKIN

There is a tale in the early 13th-century Saga of the V...lsungs that contains the wolfskin method of being a werewolf. The two young guys, Sigmund and Sinfj...tli, were walking through the woods at one point when they came across a massive home. There were two men asleep in deep sleep. The magic spell had been applied to them, causing them to seven days of wolves. On the tenth day , they were allowed to get rid of the enchanted wolfskins, which caused them to be wolves, and then become men once more.

From MEN to WEREWOLVES

The two young men opted to take the wolfskins and steal them while the other men were sleeping. They snuck in, grabbed the skins, and then fled. When they got away from the cottage , they put on the skins on and instantly transformed into the wolf. They both cried and realized that they could speak the language spoken by wolves. They agreed to separate however, they agreed that should one of them find himself being pursued with more than 7 hunters they would both howl, and the other would come to help. The next day, Sigmund encountered a group of hunters who attempted to murder him. He yelled and Sinfj...tli came in and killed the entire group of humans. After that, Sinfj...tli was attacked by eleven hunters, but he was successful in killing them all. Sigmund was on the scene accidentally and inquired about why he had not summoned Sinfj...tli. There are more than seven hunter in all. Sinfj...tli was confident, but said to Sigmund that he didn't need assistance in managing such a small group of people.

RETURNING CHANGE

Sigmund was angry by what he interpreted as an attack on his skills. He was furious and hurled himself at Sinfj...tli to bite him on the throat. After he left and his friend was lying on the ground, still in motion. Sigmund was immediately ashamed of the actions he took by putting on the wolfskin, and then attacking Sinfj...tli. He grabbed his companion and took back to his home in the woods. The house was vacant by two men. As he was walking towards the home he saw two weasels quilling. One of them bit the throat of the other and then sped off into a thicket before returning with a leaf which was thrown on the wound of other. In a flash, the weasel healed, and it appeared to be as if he'd never been injured. Sigmund set out in search of the leaf, and then an eagle appeared, with the leaf with its beak. Sigmund placed it over his friend's wound , and Sinfj...tli became healed. The tenth day after their journey, they returned to their human appearances, cut the wolfskins and put them in a fire, which reduced them to nothingness.

Transformation and Metamorphosis

There's a lot of discord in the different description of the transformation of man to wolf and in the animal that result from it. Sometimes, this transformation comes by chance, while at other times it is controlled by times of the day or the seasons. Sometimes, the creature is half-wolf, half-man or a creature that can be seen walking on its hind feet but on other occasions, it is a wolf for all ends and purposes. Even when it's killed, there is a lack of consistency. At times, it keeps its wolf-like shape while at other times it changes back to its human shape.

In its behavior like humans, there's an element of discord. Werewolves who are not changed by outside entities are not necessarily savage or cruel when they are in human form. In many stories they are gentle gentle, kind people until they transform to the form of wolves. In certain instances of metamorphosis involuntary and the majority of the time, they are voluntary. The werewolf is considered to be a bad person in the first place. as a wolf the creature is a mixture of man and beast with all his subtle wit and ability to reason.

CANNIBALISTIC TendenCIES

In search of an explanation that is rational, have suggested believing that the myth of werewolves could be linked to the need for blood that some have and is often associated with hallucinations that lead the person to believe they are wolves. They refer to tribes of cannibals from Africa who exploit their neighbors their fear of wolves to satisfy their craving for flesh and blood, by dressing in wolfskins and attacking their foes in the night, thereby generating myths about the half-eaten remains found are part of half-human Half-wolf creatures who roam in remote areas in the evening hours. So, the existence of such creatures over time, become a definite fact.

The PROCESS FOR METAMORPHOSIS

German reformer as well as scholar, doctor and physician Caspar Peucer published in the Commentarius De Praecipiuys Diuinationum Genribus of 1553:

For me, I previously considered as absurd and unbelievable the stories I heard regarding the transformation of humans to wolves, but I've learned from reliable sources and the testimony of credible witnesses that these stories aren't at all unlikely or unbelievable, as they relate of these transformations that take place 12 months after Christmas time in Livonia and other countries. They have been proven to be authentic through the confessions of people who were incarcerated and tortured in connection with such infractions. This is how the process.

When Christmas is over, a deaf boy is seen calling the slaves of Satan, among them a large number, and encouraging them to follow his lead. If they delay or move too slow, then there is a tall, muscular man holding whips that have thongs constructed of iron chains that he nudges them to move forward. Sometimes, he punishes the wretches brutally that the marks left by the whips are left on their bodies for a long time afterward, and cause the most suffering. When they embarked on their journey and have arrived, they're all transformed to wolves.

...They move in huge numbers with their conductor the person who holds the whip, following whom they move. Once they are in the field, they run at the cattle that they spot in the fields, tearing and dragging away everything they can. They also cause numerous other damages; however, they aren't allowed to hurt or touch people. When they cross any river their guide separates the water with his whip and they appear to be opening up, leaving an empty space to pass.

After twelve days, the entire band disperses and returns to their homes and regains his authentic appearance. The transformation, according to them occurs in this manner. People who have been transformed are thrown to the ground like they are afflicted with epilepsy. There they lay without movement or life. Their bodies don't leave the place where they fell, nor are their limbs transformed into the hairy limbs of Wolf, but the spirit or soul by an attraction leaves the inert body and moves into the wolf's world after which, when they have filled up with their disgusting lupine desires and lusts, through the Devilis power it re-enters the body of the previous human which is then rejuvenated by the re-emergence of the life force.

According to numerous accounts the transformation can be very painful and is often associated to the appearance of the moon as outlined by historian Gervase Tilbury. This idea was never attributed to the werewolf until it was adopted by contemporary fiction writers, probably because of the dramatic impact it created in a transition as if the idea of a human being transforming into a wolf wasn't sufficient drama.

Curse of the Werewolf

There are many reasons why one can become a werewolf and inflicting offenses in the name of God and then being excommunicated is just one. The story tells from the perspective of Hugues III of Campdavaine, the count of Saint-Pol in the region that is part of Somme located in north France which destroyed Abbey of Saint-Riquier by killing the clergy who were inside as well as a lot of individuals who were sheltered within the walls. He was in agreement to Pope Innocent III to pay for his guilt by building three abbeys. But it appears that this wasn't enough to make up for his sins. When he passed away in 1141 the ghost of his deceased was frequently observed in the form of a wolf in black, shaking heavy chains of metal which weighed him down crying as he wandered around the Saint-Riquier abbey.

The King John in England was another instance of a monarch who was excommunicated by that similar pope Innocent III. His ghost also was observed as a lupine even after his death. The legend of the loup-garou in France it was believed that the loup-garou could be an act of metamorphosis that was forced on an unidentified condemned person who, being tortured within his tomb, was able to tear his way out. The initial stage of the process was to eat the cerecloth that surrounded his face. Then, as his screams and muffled howls came from the tomb, in the darkness of night, the ground of the tomb was beginning to rise then the scream came out, with a dazzling stare, emitting a smell that was fetid, it emerged from the grave like the wolf.

The CURSE OF SEVEN

The region of East Friesland, it is believed that if seven girls are paired up within a family, one of them will definitely become a werewolf. It is no surprise that young men might be reluctant to marry one of the seven sisters. There is also a legend seven sons of seventh was turned into a werewolf. This is the story that is believed in Galician, Portuguese and Brazilian folklore. This belief was also propagated by the northern region of Argentina in which the werewolf was called the Lobizon. To avoid being a werewolf in the family, the seventh child of the seventh was usually abandoned following birth, or killed, or given away to those who had no knowledge of the history of the child.

INVOLUNTARY WEREWOLVES

People who are evil, such as sorcerers and witches may be turned into werewolves in order to commit crimes of violence as well as create involuntary werewolves through casting spells on innocents. Some people also become involuntary werewolves due to being born in the wrong place like when the moon is full or due to being afflicted by epilepsy or other illnesses. For instance, in Campania in Italy there is a belief that any person born on Christmas night is likely to become a werewolf for the rest of their life. Likewise, in Sicily this fate was believed to be attributed to people born during a new moon.

Silver Bullets & Wolfsbane

One of the best ways to deter someone from being a werewolf was to kill him. And, according to some reports it could be done with the silver bullet. Other, more effective, but often odd methods include getting rid of the wolfskin girdle or girdle; cutting off a limb, which causes the creature to change back to human form, sitting in one place for 100 years, being accused of being waswolf-like, being greeted by the cross symbol as well as getting addressed 3 times with your baptismal name, getting struck three times on your forehead by a knife or having at minimum three droplets of blood taken out of the body victim person.

Folklore tells about throwing an iron rod at a werewolf in order to make him return to his human. Similar to a vampire striking a stake into the center of a werewolf can put an end to its actions. A sword blessed at an altar in a church dedicating itself to Saint Hubert could be employed to kill a waswolf. The only sure way to eliminate the werewolf and ensure it is not successful in reviving or becoming vampire is to sever the head, the heart, or even its entire body.

ST THOMAS AQUINAS

The power of turning other people to wild animals was believed to be not just to wicked witches, sorcerers, and demons, but also to Christian saints. As a theologian and philosopher, St Thomas Aquinas wrote, All angels, good and bad , possess the ability of transmuting our bodies. The tale is told about St Patrick for example in the long-standing Norse text known as"Konungs Skuggsja: Konungs Skuggsja:

There's another marvel in the country that could be quite unbelievable; however the people who live in the area believe in that it is true and attribute it to the fury of the holy man. The story goes that when the saintly Patricus taught Christianity in the country There was one clan that was more obstinately opposed to him that any other clan in the country They strove to slander him in a variety of ways, both in a way that was disrespectful to God in addition to to the saintly man. While he was preaching the Gospel to them in the same way as to other people and went to discuss matters with them, where they held their gatherings, they made a plan of screaming at them like the wolves. As he realized that he was able to do little to spread his message to the people he was extremely angry and prayed to God to send a curse on them that would be passed on to their descendants to serve as a constant reminder of their indifference. In the end, these clansmen suffered an appropriate and severe, but extremely awe-inspiring punishment, as it is said that the entire clan members change into the wolf for a time and are able to roam the woods, eating the same foods as the wolves, but they are more dangerous than wolves, as even in their devious ways they possess the same wit as men, even though they're just equally eager to devour humans and other animals. The story goes that the affliction occurs every seventh winter, but over the course of time, they're men. Others endure it through seven winters, and never again struck.

According to legend, St. Patrick also punishes the Welsh King Vereticus by making Vereticus and his followers into wolves when they refused to follow the doctrines of Christianity. The St Columba's disciple St Columba, St Natalis was believed to have placed curses upon an elite Irish family which resulted in that everyone in the family was turned into a the wolf for seven years, and was confined to the woods. In fact The 1188 Topographica Hibernica written by medieval theologian and clergyman, Giraldus Cambrensis, relates an account of a priest who was conversing with a wolf that had been cursed by fate.

St Augustine wrote of werewolves in a modern way and almost in agreement with psychiatrists of today in his assertion that even though people might not physically transform to werewolves, they believe in their thoughts that they're.

It is widely believed that with certain witchesi curses or the influence of the Devil people can be transformed into the form of wolves... However, they don't lose their human logic and sense of humour and are not changed to the level of a beast. This must be taken in the following manner: namely that the Devil is not able to create a new form of nature and is able to create an appearance that actually isn't. Because by no magic or any evil force will the mind, not even and not even the body itself change into the physical features and limbs of any animal...but the human being is inexplicably and in the illusion of metamorphosing into an animal, even though it appears to be the form of a quadruped.

He stated this in order to prove that only God could create physical creatures, whether animals or humans. The devil was merely able to create an illusion. Even though he's never depicted in the form of a quadruped the Christian Saint Christopher is to west-coast Christians as the saint patron of travelers is often depicted in Orthodox art, depicting the head of an animal. Could he be a werewolf?

ST   CHRISTOPHER   DOG-HEADED   ST
CHRISTOPHER THE DOG-HEADED

Legend says that in the year 300 AD in the year 300 AD, the Romans were able to capture Reprobus who was a soldier from the Berber Marmaritae tribe of Cyrene located west of Egypt. The Marmaritae were frequently described as a cannibalistic, dog-headed tribe. Like many captive soldiers Reprobus got drafted in the Roman army. He also was converted to Christianity and adopted the name Christopher which means 'bearer Christ'. When he was taken by the city of Antioch in Syria He started to help convert others to Christianity as well. He was successful that he was even sentenced to be executed. St Christopher wasn't was a werewolf However, he was not a werewolf. He was not was a cannibal with a dog's head, except in the sense that the term "dog-headed cannibal" was a term used in the Greco-Roman period of the abuse of those who were not part of the Roman Empire and, in particular, Africans. There is no doubt that the term was associated in his honor by the scribes who wrote the first stories of his life. It was also accepted in later writings as an accurate description of his appearance.

Chapter 5: The Werewolf Slaying

Silver is regarded as a sacred metal with purifying properties. If it is in the presence of a werewolf it can burn into the flesh of the animal and also weaken it and make it difficult to recognize. It is important to note that the item does not have to be a bullet made of silver. Any silver item that is embedded into the flesh of the animal will burn through the hairy layers. There's some debate as to whether a bullet made of silver will kill the werewolf however there is one thing that is certain that silver is the main foe of the werewolf. Hence, make sure you have it with you always.

SURVIVING A WEREWOLF

Quicksilver (a liquid alloy of silver and mercury) is believed to have the ability to destroy the heart of a werewolf if they inject it into the bloodstream. The religious symbols are known to ward off all supernatural evil like vampires, witches and of course, werewolves. A silver cross can be extremely powerful. If you're feeling under threat, it's worthwhile to carry a holy host in your bag, in the shape of a bottle of holy water or communion wine sprinkle it all over the predator to cause fatal consequences. There is also a belief that the Greek or Turkish Eye charm is anathema to Lycanthrops. They have a tendency to dislike trees like mountain Ash and rye, so mistletoe and wolfsbane are utilized to deter attacks. The golden rule of killing is that the brain or the heart must be destroyed for an animal to remain dead. Other wounds will quickly heal over the course of an entire day and the werewolf will be able to hunt once more.

BERNARD VERLAND

A tale from the early 20th century is about an unnamed young man Bernard Verland who, while walking through the Ardennes Mountains of Belgium was confronted by three suspicious-looking men with eyebrows that matched on the bridge of their noses. It was an obvious signal of werewolves taking on human form. Bernard's dog was agitated and roared at the men and appeared to be scared of them.

Bernard continued to walk, however he was aware that three men were a short distance to him. He increased his speed. After a short time He arrived at an unlit, dark spot where the trees grew close to each other. At once, the dog sped off , and Bernard was right behind him. As he ran, Bernard could hear howling dogs and footsteps rushing following him. The more quickly he ran and the further the footsteps seemed to appear. He was unsure of what he could do to avoid them and was reminded of being told about the fact that the mountain-ash tree is capable of protecting against some types of evil creatures or demons. He looked around and saw one in the distance and jumped onto its trunk and climbed through the branches below as swiftly as possible. He sat in the tree, hoping that whatever creature were following him would react negatively to this particular kind of tree. He looked around, and the three werewolves gathered on the scene, however they abruptly stopped at its bottom. They were looking around, snarling in anger, but refused to even attempt to get close to the tree or even attempt at climbing up it. They yelled in frustration, before turning around and to his delight the tree was smashed away.

STOPPING A ATTACK

Werewolves can be snuffed out of their snare by being cut in the forehead or struck at least three times, with something sharp, making sure blood flow is drawn. If you're facing an attack that is full-frontal by a vicious snarling werewolf it is possible to not do so however, the drawing of three droplets of blood off the animal using a needle can halt any attack. Of course one of the most effective tips if you wish to stay safe from werewolf-related attacks is to avoid dark forests and dark woods, particularly, when the moon is full.

"The Rise of the Werewolf Myth

They believe that the belief of werewolves comes in part, according to some from the impression imposed by man in the past by the powerful elements of the natural world. All things changed - sun moon and wind, as well as weather. the seasons, and the cycle of life brought about the most dramatic changes in the stages of birth, adolescence, and death. Gods too changed, adopting various forms according to what was best for them . Poseidon Jupiter Ammon Milosh Kobilitch Minerva among many other.

If these all changed and the human race was able to adapt, why shouldn't it as well. Particularly, if the alteration could serve as a reason for the inhumanity that is a part of society, be it an serial killer or serial rapist, at any time in time. Some people have propose other reasons for the widespread werewolf fear that took over Europe for a few years. One theory centers around poisoning caused by ergot. Ergot is a kind of fungus that thrives on the grains of rye in certain circumstances, typically in wet seasons following the cold winter. It is a source of alkaloids that could cause the condition known as ergotism , which affects mammals and humans that consume grain. The illness has been suggested as a plausible explanation for potential cases of werewolfism in Europe during the 18th and 19th centuries.

The signs of ergotism include symptoms of diarrhea, spasms as well as paraesthesias (tingling or numbness in the skin) and nausea, headaches and vomiting. But, there may be hallucinations believed to be similar to those caused by the ingestion of the psychedelic substance, LSD, which can actually come from the ergot. Psychosis and mania are usually apparent. Ergot poisoning is blamed for people believing that they were werewolves, and to cause a hysteria epidemic in towns that cause people to believe they've seen the werewolf.

Of of course, there are plenty of different reasons why people blame violent, bizarre circumstances and incidents on supernatural causes like werewolves. The serial killing or rape, or cannibalism and cannibalism are all difficult to comprehend as an act of someone within your own neighborhood. What better way of convincing all people that the problem within the town or village is not a result of human nature than to identify a scapegoat like the werewolf. It was convenient also to blame the strange ailments that cause people to behave in a bizarre, unsocial manner on the simple victim of the werewolf which is controlled by invisible external forces.

MADNESS and SSHAPESHIFTING

The ancients came up with the terms boanthropy, kuanthropy, or lycanthrop to refer to a kind of mental illness that caused a person to believe themselves to have a form, with each one of these indicating a different form in which the person believes they have been transformed - a wolf the dog, or a cow or a cow, for instance. In other regions of the world, animals from local areas were used as models for changing shape. In Europe bears were often the most preferred form, and in Africa the hyena, or the leopard were the most popular choices. In the past, Khands of India talked of wer-tigers like the people from the rainforests of Java as well as Sumatra. In Arawak there was a legend that wer-jaguars used to wander the hills.

Ancient Beliefs

The myth of the werewolf's origins are from Greek mythology. The first werewolf was believed to be Lycaon who was from Arcadia located in Peloponnese. The story of Lycaon was published at the end of the 2nd century by Greek biographer and traveler Pausanias as part of Pausanias's Eighth Book of his Description of Greece.

ZEUS and LYCAON

In the past, many were believed to worship Prometheus instead of the goddesses and gods of Mount Olympus. Lycaon was adamantly hostile towards his fellow Olympians who were under the direction of

Zeus by blaming them and blaspheming them. Infuriated by Lycaon's behaviour, Zeus resolved to teach him the lesson. He went to the home of Lycaon to convince him that he was in error. Lycaon invited him to his home and assured him that the man that he would listen. The king invited Zeus to a meal to discuss what he could accomplish to win the respect of gods. The confident Lycaon was not planning on engaging in a debate with Zeus however. Instead, he chose to fool Zeus. He was in a dungeon at his home that was full of people who had wronged him , and who he was wealthy and powerful enough to control. He picked one of the prisoners and demanded that his throat be cut , and his flesh be cooked in the stew to be consumed that evening.

A GREAT MEAL

The meal was set on the table, and Lycaon and Zeus were seated to take their meals. Zeus however being omniscient, and recognizing immediately the mistake Lycaon did was furious and dropped the food into the air. Incredulous that his plot was discovered, Lycaon leapt to his feet and attempted to flee. While he fled but was surprised to discover that something was occurring to his body. His frantic cries transformed into snarls and growls. was able to get down to all fours and started running. His nose turned to a snout, and his ears expanded until they became directed. The teeth of his mouth grew into fangs, and the most bizarre of all hair, thick and dense began to grow across the body.

HIS STORY IS SEALED

There is a legend that Lycaon was the one who had the final laugh because, being an unmistakably bloodthirsty kind of guy and a lover of werewolves, he adored the role of a werewolf. This allowed him to slaughter humans, goats, and sheep in the manner he desired. In the end, however locals grew were fed up with his actions and he was banished to Tatarus. The transformation of Lycaon wasn't permanent, but in the event that he could not eat meat for nine consecutive years. If he gave in to the temptation to eat flesh of a human, the wolf would be an omnivore for all time. Lycaon is believed to have been an wolf for the rest of his existence.

In the Book I of the Metamorphoses the famous Roman poet Ovid wrote of Lycaon:

He was unsuccessful in his attempts to speak. He stopped speaking at the moment he realised

His jaws were filled with foam, but only did he spit out

For blood, he ran amid the hordes of cattle and cried out to eat.

His vesture changed into hair; his limbs turned curly;

A wolf, he still has a significant evidence of his early expression

Hoary is he as before his face is savage,

The eyes of his mate sparkle fiercely in a picture of sheer the fury.

Naturally, as a group of people living off the landscape in the rural areas they suffered heavily from wolves' attacks, their escape was secured according to them, through the sacrifice of the child. The practice was first introduced by Lycaon and it is likely that it was not just the term lycanthropy but the whole story was created by him.

NEURI TRIBE

The history of ancient Greece also tells us the history about the Neuri tribe that were believed to change form into an animal every year. The Neuri were found throughout the Bug River basin to the west of the Dnieper which is roughly in the present-day region of Poland in Poland and Belarus. They were believed to have practiced sorcery. However, they were skeptical of the Greek scholar, Herodotus of Halicarnassus, did not believe they had power to change shape.

It is believed to me that Neuri are witches, and as that they are believed to be by Scythians and also by the Greek inhabitants of Scythie who claimed that each year, at least one Neurian is transformed into a wolf some time and back to his former form. But, this is not something they can convince me to believe in their claims, even though they make it clear and confirm it with swearing in a solemn oath.

ODYSSEY

Homer In the Odyssey composed around 8th century BC recounts the tale of the journey over ten years in the life of Trojan War hero, Odysseus.

At some point, Odysseus observes smoke rising from the trees on tiny island. He and his companions draw lots to determine who is going into the forest to study. 23 of his men go out and , after a short time, arrive at a stone structure which is in the midst of mountain lions and wolves. As soon as they spot the men the animals leap up and begin to run towards them however, they don't attack. They slow down and stroll towards them , waving their tails like domestic animals. These are men who have entered the home of the gorgeous goddess Circe who turned them into were-lions and werewolves. Although they possess the body of animals, they have the minds of human beings and are delighted to meet people who are also human.

A DANGEROUS TRAP

The animals can't explain this to the men of Odysseus who are captivated by the gorgeous song of the enchantress Circe. They are welcomed to her house and cooks food, however the food contains a poison that makes them forget their home. The witch raises her hand since she's the god of magical and transforms the swine into swine. In this state they are taken outside to join the rest of the animals. One of them escapes however, and returns to the ship in order to tell Odysseus the story of what transpired. Odysseus angry that he has seemingly lost his men is sent out with a group to rescue the prisoners. While on the way, he's fortunate enough to be spotted by God Hermes who supplies him with an herb that's an alternative to Circe's drug. It is known as'moly' and is a black root with an white flower.

A CREEPY Trick

The gorgeous Circe will welcome the legendary hero into her home , and she serves him a drink in a gold cup. Unbeknownst to him she pours in the poison she's already fed to his soldiers. He drinks it , and Circe creates her wand ready to turn him into an animal. However, she is confused there is nothing to happen. Odysseus is taking the magical herb that was given by Hermes. Odysseus jumps up, with his sword ready However, in that instant, Circe falls head-over-heels in the love of him and offers him to sleep with her. Prior to accepting but he insists upon her swearing to not hurt him.

Then, Odysseus asks her to liberate their men of the swine-like spell she has imposed on them. She obliges by brewing a potion that restores them to human form, and brings back their memories that they lost. In addition it makes them appear younger than they did before. They leave and leave Circe on her magical island with her were-lion and were-wolf and were-lion companions.

PETRONIUS

The first century Roman writer, Petronius wrote the following tale in his hilarious book, The Satyricon. It was written from the perspective of an ex-slave Niceros during the dinner party of Trimalcio, his best friend. Trimalcio:

My master had travelled to Capua to market some of his old clothes. I had the chance to persuade him to stay with me for about five miles outside town, for he was a soldier and as courageous as death. We set out in search of the cockcrows, and the moon was as bright as a day while we were passing by the monuments of my friend, he began to speak to the stars while I was jogging along, singing and noting them. Then I looked back at him I saw him strip his clothes and put his clothes on the roadside. My heart was pounding within a moment, and I was like a corpse and then, through an instant, he transformed into an Wolf. Don't think I'm making fun of myself I will not say a lie to gain one of the greatest fortunes that exists.

To continue: once his transformation into the wolf, he started to growl and headed toward the woods. At first , I didn't know if I was standing in my head or on my back; but when I was when I finally got to pick off his clothes I discovered that they had been turned into stones. The sweat poured out of me and I didn't expect to be able to overcome it. Melissa started to question why I was walking so late. If you had arrived a bit earlier, she added, you could have at least offered us a hand. For an animal broke into our farm and killed our livestock; however, even though he was able to escape and was not a laughing matter for himas one of our employees chased him over with the help of a pike.i Upon hearing this, I was unable to shut my eye; however, when it became daylight, I left as a pedlar having been released from his burden. As I walked to the spot that the clothes were transformed into stone, I found nothing more than a pool of blood when I arrived home, I discovered my soldier in bed with an ox an stall, and an ophthalmologist was dressed his neck. I was immediately aware that he was a man who was able to change his skin and I would never take bread from his family, except in the event that you had killed me. Anyone who has another view on the matter are invited to voice have their say; however, if I lie to you and you believe me, let your guardian spirits bewilder me!

The Festival of the Wolf

The Lupercalia is also known as the Festival of the Wolf, was celebrated in Rome each year during the past between February 13 and 15. It was essentially a festival of shepherds. It was staged to honor Faunus the god of horns of the plains, forest and fields. He represents the Roman equivalent to Pant, the Greek god Pan. An image of Faunus was erected at the Lupercal. In this festival, sacrifices were performed by two goats and a dog. There was a feast as the goatskins were cut up into pieces, which they Luperci (Brothers of the Wolf) were able to wear around themselves like an apron, after having removed their clothes. With the help of a brother, they walked around the city wall that was once in place with naked men being encouraged by women and girls who lined the course. Each brother held a piece of goatskin which used to whip women who fought with each other to get the men's attention. The goatskin was thought to held the power of gods and that any woman who was that was touched by it would quickly become pregnant and receive the swift and safe delivery of a child.

The Romans used a term for changing shape - versipellis. This literally means "turning the skin'. However it could also be used to refer to'sly or cunning. From it, come the English words 'turncoat' and "turnskin" to describe those who change sides.

These tales, specifically those that tell the tale of Lycaon are transmitted through time and rewritten by the storytellers for their own advantage. It is for this reason that they must be treated with a pinch salt. But, it is true that earliest roots of the folklore of the werewolf stretch deep into the shadows of the past provides comfort to those who believe in the supernatural and provides nonbelievers with an intriguing understanding of the development of a myth.

MARCELLUS SIDETES

The second century Roman poet Marcellus Sidetes wrote a long medical poem in Greek the hexameter form from which fragments survive. One poem, titled De Lycanthropia, claimed that the lycanthropy-induced madness affected all people at the beginning of the new year. He wrote about how the insanity and the rage would grow more severe in February, and how sufferers would sleep in graveyards that were abysmal, hiding in the darkness like ravening wolves and dogs.

People suffering from the illness of lycanthropy are out at night during february, in imitation of dogs or wolves in all aspects and tend to stay in tombs until the dawn.

These are the signs which will help you discern the sufferers of this illness. They look pale and their gaze is drowsy and their eyes are dry and do not make tears. You can see that their eyes are sunken , their tongues are dry and they're in a state of not being able to gain the weight. They are thirsty and their shins are covered with cuts that are not healing because they're constantly falling and getting attacked by dogs. This is the reason they are suffering.

It is important to recognize the fact that lycanthropy can be a manifestation of melancholia. It is treated by opening an incision when it is manifestation and removing it until moment of falling asleep. Then, feed the patient food that is conducive to a good mood. The patient will be treated to sweet baths. Following that by using the whey of the milk, wash his body over three days with the gourd-medicine Rufus and Archigenes as well as Justus. Repeat this process a third or second time at intervals.

Following the purifications, one can take the antidote against bites from vipers. Also, take the other steps recommended earlier to treat melancholia. When the evening approaches and melancholia begins to manifest apply to the head the lotions that are known to help to induce sleep. You can also anoint your nostrils with scents like these kinds and the opium. Sometimes, offer sleep-inducing drinks as well.

The famous Roman poet Virgil composed:

These herbs of a curse for me did Moeris offer,

In Pontus the weeds are trimmed, and where a myriad of plants abound.

Through these full oft have I witnessed Moeris alter

to morph into a wolf and then hide him in the woods

The most frequent summoning of spirits is through the recesses of tombs.

To new fields, you can move the corn that is standing.

The mythology world is filled with characters who transformed into beasts of various kinds for example: Jupiter transformed into a bull Hecuba changed into a bitch Actaeon changed into a stag Ulysses friends were transformed into swine , and the daughters of Proetus were able to run through the fields, believing they had become cows. So convinced were they that they were hesitant to allow anyone to come near them in the event that they were to were to put a yoke upon their backs.

PLINY THE ELDER

Pliny the Elder was a writer who lived from 23 to was 79 years old was a writer who composed about the werewolves within the book Eight of his vast writings, Natural History (Historia Naturalis) and cited his Greek writer Euanthes as the basis for the Arcadian tale. Pliny provides a version of the story where one of the members of the family of Anthus was selected by a lot each year, and then took to a lake. There, the man stripped himself and put his clothes on the oak tree. Then he swam across the water , and on the opposite side, was transformed into Wolf. The next nine years as an group of wolves. If he could successfully stay away from contact with human beings for nine years, the wolf was able to go back into the water, swim across it and come back, regaining his human appearance.

Pliny also mentions an author called Agriopas who wrote the story of Demaenetus of Parrhasia who was a wolf during the Arcadian sacrifices in celebration of Zeus Lycaeus's celebration was a wolf who ate the intestines of a human infant and then was transformed into an wolf for the duration of 10 years to be punished. He reverted to his human form at conclusion of the ten years and even participated at the Olympic Games. Pliny however was adamantly skeptical of the concept of werewolves including it with a host of other myths that were eventually proved to be untrue. However, he did acknowledge that, however that many people believed that werewolves existed and believed in the possibility of experiencing the phenomenon of versipellis ('changing one's appearance of the skin').

ROMULUS AND REMUS

A story that is among the most well-known of all tales about wolves is that of wild children, Romulus and Remus, mythical creators for the town of Rome. According to the account of Livy, the Roman historian Livy (c.59 17bc) within his work The History of Rome (called by his Ab Urbe Condita, meaning "From the City that Has been Founded') Mars, the Roman god of war, imposes himself on Rhea Silvia, the Vestal Virgin, Rhea Silvia who is conceived by him, despite the fact Vestal Virgins weren't supposed to have children or marry. The priestess is detained and is subsequently born two sons known as Romulus and Remus in the 771st year of BC.

The King, Amulius, who has removed Rhea Silvia's dad, is worried of the possibility that both boys become teenagers and fight to the crown. Amulius therefore orders to drown them within the River Tiber. When the time comes however the river is already at its highest level and the deepest portion of the river is not reached (some versions depict them floating in a vessel before being washed up on the shore). Instead of drowning and buried, the twins are thrown into the shade of a fallen fig tree. The twins' crying cries can be heard from a wolf who is at the riverbank to drink . in lieu of killing the twins she comforts the twins and feeds them the milk of her personal. The she-wolf is assisted by a woodpecker who offers them food. The woodpecker and the she-wolf curiously, were both animals that were that were sacred to Mars. In the past, she carried twins of her own to a cave that is now known as the "Lupercal which is located on the Palatine Hill, on which Rome was established.

The twins are discovered by Faustulus who is a shepherd who returns them and his wife Acca Larentia and raises them like they are her own. When they reach the age of adulthood they kill Amulius, the usurper and restore their father, Numitor, as king of Alba Longa. They decide later to establish their own city, and select as their location the place that the she-wolf cared for them in The

Palatine Hill. When they begin building the city, they split up - some sources suggest that this is due to the fact that Remus took a sly swipe at the walls Romulus had been building. They fight, and Romulus murders his brother. However, Romulus continues to build the city, and named the city Roma (Rome) in honor of his own name.

WEREWOLF LEGENDS

Britain and Ireland

In England the werewolf myths faded away as wolves became extinct in the countryside. King Edgar who reigned between 959 and 975, was credited with the eradication of England of the wolves. He changed the annual payment that he received from the King Idwall of Wales usually lavish and gold-plated in 300 wolf pelts. It is claimed that in the span of four years, there were no living wolves. However, the complete extermination of wolves may not happen until later. Actually the last wolf that lived in England is believed to have been killed during the 15th century in Wormhill within Derbyshire.

King John The ZOMBIE-WEREWOLF

One tale concerns the royal personality that was not popular King John who was also often referred to as John "Lackland" because, as the son of his father's oldest the king did not get the land that was part of the estates of his family and, as king, he was able to lose significant areas of his territory to the French. John stole from many monasteries and churches during his reign. In one of them, the Cistercian Abbey in Swineshead near Bolton He gorged himself on peaches believed to be taken by an monk as revenge for the wrongs caused to the Catholic Church. Dysentery was a problem for him, John was taken to Newark where he passed away. In accordance with his wishes, John was laid to rest at the altar at Worcester Cathedral, between the shrines of two English saints, Oswald and Wulfstan. After his burial the public was shocked to hear loud screams and howls coming from the tomb. It was the Canons of Worcester decided to stop the horrible noise and had the body exhumed, and then reburied in unconsecrated ground.

Much to their dismay To their great disappointment, this didn't mean that the issue was over. It appears that the king was not going to lie in his new tomb. The media reported on his disgusting decaying corpse roaming the fields like a werewolf, terrorizing anyone who crossed his way.

THE BLACK BEAST of SCOTLAND

The last wolf that roamed the hills of Scotland has been believed to be dead in 1743, near Pall-a-chrocain located in Tarnaway Forest in Moray. A "black beast" had killed two children and a mother and prompted the local laird to bring for a hunter who was well-known, named MacQueen. When the day was set for to hunt for the beast, MacQueen's laird as well as his followers waited for hours for the hunter of fame to show up. He finally showed up to the disgruntled faces and inquired why they were so frustrated. After that, he smiled, opened the bag and took out that bloody head which was responsible for killing the woman and her kids.

The first werewolf of MERIONETHSHIRE

The county that was once Merionethshire located in northwest Wales appears to have been the home of more than two werewolves. One tale from the 1930s tells of the Oxford professor as well as his spouse who lived in an unassuming cottage in the county. When they were swimming in the lake in front of his cottage, the teacher stumbled upon an animal skull that appeared be a large dog-like animal. The professor took the animal home and set it on an island within the kitchen.

A few days later, the couple was hosting a guest, and the professor as well as their guest took an excursion with the woman at the house. There was a feeling of unease about the skull , and her fear was heightened when she heard a squealing sound coming from the kitchen door. She was thinking it would be prudent to walk into the kitchen and secure the door however, as she was about to do so she was astonished by the appearance of a person in the window. It was the shape of a man. However, its hairy body. And it was a face with the angry eyes like a wolf. The worst part was that it seemed like it tried to gain entry in the cabin. Luckily, the professor and their guest arrived at the right time, and the creature vanished. When the woman in a shaking state revealed what she had witnessed the night before, they decided to take up arms with a shotgun before getting some clubs.

CONFRONTED BY THE BEAST

After a few hours, they noticed a scratching sound at the window of the kitchen. They jumped to their feet and looked up to find themselves looking at the eyes of a werewolf glowing with bloodlust. But it turned around and fled after it saw them, and began to pursue it. They were amazed when it appeared to glide across the ground at a speed, which was way too speedy for them. It headed towards the lake but disappeared and did not cause a splash or ripple as it was able to enter the water. The next day, around dawn the professor was able to return his skull back to its exact location in the lake in which the body was discovered. The werewolf did not return.

THE SECOND WEREWOLF of MERIONETHSHIRE

Miss St Denis was an artist who lived on the farm. She had a habit that she would set up her art easel up in the local railway station since the platform provided the most ideal location for drawing or painting the surrounding countryside. The station was small that had only one platform, and a basic box to serve as a waiting area and the booking office. The station's functions were carried out by one person, and this was all it took as trains slowed down very frequently.

A SPOOKY ENCOUNTER

A few hours earlier, she'd been focused on her work and had a hard time remembering to see what the current time was. As she looked up at the sky, she realized it was earlier than usual and that it was going to get dark, she quickly began packing her belongings. When she was done but she was astonished to find a man sitting on a truck just a couple of yards away, gazing at her. There was no one within the vicinity of the station, unless on the rare occasion that trains were arriving, and the last thing she was aware it was not a train scheduled at that moment.

An UNEASY sensation

She was suddenly worried. The house of the station master was only a few hundred yards away. Beyond her home at the farm was the closest safest place. Invoking all her strength to ask the gentleman if he could inform her of what time it was and he was in silence, looking at her in the dark darkness. She quickly put the items away, put her belongings, went out of the gate and began to leave the station and attempted to appear as relaxed to the situation. A bit further while walking she glanced at her shoulder. In shock she noticed that a person was standing behind her. She increased her speed and started to whine and try to appear as calm and unaffected as is possible. She continued walking along with him. She knew that a short distance from the road, the road would be surrounded by cliffs on either side, turning the road black and closing her out. In a moment of determination she turned around and shouted, "What do you really want? You're a fool! But the words fell off her lips as an abrupt flash of light swung across the figure and the scene made her tremble.

A SURPRISE MOVEMENT

The creature was a head of a wild wolf with shaggy grey fur. The creature opened the mouth, and displayed long white teeth. It sank back with a crouch and was poised to attack. It was Miss St Denis suddenly remembered that in her purse was a flashlight which she had in case of emergency. She looked around in her bag and found it, taking it out, and turning it on when the creature surged into the air. The light immediately had an impact. The creature slowed down in fear, and then threw its hands like paws over its eyes to block out the light. While doing this it sat there, then mysteriously, disappeared to nothing. It was Miss St Denis never saw the werewolf in the following night, but she did inquire about the locals shortly afterward. She discovered that in one quarry near the spot in which she saw the werewolf, strange bones were discovered that are believed to be human , and partly animal.

IRAN

Ireland also has its own stories of werewolves, dating all the way all the way back St Patrick himself. In Ireland in order to be a werewolf, a person didn't have to undergo a curse or make an arrangement in with Satan. It was simply a matter of being born into a family who contained blood from a werewolf coursing into its veins. It was officially recognized too. It was recognized by the Late Middle Irish treatise on names The Coir Anmann (Fitness of Names) includes a specific Laignech Faelad that, the book states, was known to transform into Faelad (wolf shape). It also mentions that he and his

103

children, and others who later on, used to change into wolf-like shapes and killed the herds. He was named Laignech Faelad due to the fact that he was the first to transform into a wolf-like shape.'

A Norse text, called the Konungs Skuggsja, written around 1250, to help educate princes from the royal line, relates the amazing things to be found in Ireland. It describes an animal that was caught in the forest , the nature of which it was impossible to say the certainty of whether it was human or another animal. No one could understand a word spoken by it or determine if it could understand human speech. It was human-like however, in every aspect, with regard to hands, feet, but the whole body was covered in hair, as beasts do and down the back, it had hair that was coarse and long, similar to those of horses, that fell down both sides , and then dragged across the ground whenever the creature was walking. The final Irish wolf was killed 1786. The wolf was hunted down close to Mount Leinster in County Carlow after killing a few sheep. However, while wolves have ceased to pose a threat to people who were going through their day-to-day business there are still stories of werewolves from this region.

Chapter 6: Native American Werewolves

The wolf is an animal that is sacred to a variety of Native American tribes, featuring in a variety of myths and legends and rituals and songs. The wolf is viewed in a different way as opposed to the 'big bad wolf' that is so common in European stories. The story of the wolf in Native American myth the wolf is often viewed as wise and powerful , rather than as threatening and evil. For certain tribes, such as Arikara and the Shoshone and Arikara the Wolf is a creator spirit that is responsible for bringing humanity to existence. Some tell stories about the wolf saving people by teaching them the skills needed to live.

COYOTE

Alongside the wolf is often the coyote. It is often portrayed in the role of the wild wolf's naughty brother. It is also a "trickster spirit that uses tricks and deceit to accomplish his goal which is usually to expose the weaknesses of humans. Like many Native American spirits, he is able to transform to any form he wishes. The deep-seated belief in shapeshifters with a long-standing reverence for the wolf, make Native American legends a fertile place to hunt for those who have an interest in werewolves.

SKINWALKERS

A lot of Native American tribes share a belief in evil witches who are able to change their appearance at will. Skinwalkers are featured most prominently in the mythologies of tribes from the southwest, and are specifically connected to the Navajo and the Navajo, who refer to them as Yee Naaldooshi (or "they that walk on four legs'). While the definition of a Skinwalker can differ from one version to the next, there's certain things all tribes seem to be on the same page about. The first is that Skinwalkers typically wear coyote or wolf skins, making them appear similar to werewolves (they are often called 'Navajo Wolves'). Also, a chance encounter with Skinwalkers is extremely bad news.

The mere mention of Skinwalkers can be considered to be dangerous this is among the reasons why details about them are difficult to find. For the Navajo the practice of the practice of witchcraft (or"adishgash") is a real aspect of their life, and many are reluctant to take photos in case they believe that the photograph will be intended to harm them by'sympathetic magic'. They believe that talking about an item out loud could result in it happening. The most fearsome witch can be described as the Skinwalker. Moreover, since as the Navajo reside on the path of Skinwalkers, it's not that it is not surprising that there is a lack of willingness to speak about them to strangers.

The legend goes that in order in order to be a Skinwalker the witch first has to take out a blood relation with sorcery and then consume the flesh of the dead. Following this, the witch can transform into whatever animal they want and acquire the speed, strength and killing power of whatever animal they decide to transform into. They are thought to be uncaring, selfish and duplicitous and commit acts of malice solely for the sake of malice. In the daytime the Skinwalker may appear like anyone else but the eyes of their reflection reflect light in the same way as the eyes of a wolf. In the night, their eyes are not reflected by light, which is a way to differentiate them against wild animal.

CORPSE POWDER

Many believe that their eyes are glowing in the night with a yellow or red glow when they gaze is drawn to yours, then they're bound to murder you. Death can occur in a manner - Skinwalkers can berate their victim, gain the control over their victim to make them self-destruct, or break their victims up with claws resembling wolf claws. Additionally, they are believed to carry corpse dust which is made of the crushed bones of the deceased. If this powder blows into the face of a victim, they will suffer violent convulsions that will eventually kill the victim. What's good for people who don't have Navajo Blood is the fact that they are thought to attack only those who are Navajo themselves. There have been numerous stories of encounters with fierce creatures that roam the dark on land which was the property of Native Americans. If the creatures of the night are indeed Skinwalkers, they haven't been told by anyone them what kind of humans they are allowed to and should not attack.

There are obvious parallels between claims of sightings of Skinwalkers, and the reports of encounters with the other well-known North American wild-man creature, the Sasquatch or "Bigfoot". In fact, many believe that the

Sasquatch is an animal Skinwalker that takes its form as an bear or ape. Some have gone as in claiming that another paranormal phenomenon could be the result of these witches who transform into shape and Skinwalkers changing into bats or birds have even been mentioned as a possible explanation for sightings of flying objects that are not identified.

CHINDI

The Navajo believe that a Chindi is released when someone breathes their last breath. It is akin to a ghost. it's a spirit who is a representation of everything bad regarding the deceased person. died. The evil spirit is believed to be capable of causing illness and death in other. The Navajo usually attempt to ensure that the death is outdoors, allowing for the Chindi to disperse. Sometimes, they even consider burning the remains of the deceased to ensure that the Chindi does not have anything to inhabit or spread. If a death takes place in an apartment, the house is usually abandoned.

Have you ever seen a werewolf? Look closer, and it could prove as a Chindi. There are reports that suggest that the Chindi could be a part of inside the animal's body and the most likely form it would decide to adopt is that of the passing coyote or wolf. Like other Native American beliefs, details regarding the Chindi are difficult to determine because very only a few people who believe in them would like to talk about them publicly. It is believed to draw unwanted interest from Chindi. If you suspect that you're in the presence of the Chindi but you are not sure you could try drawing circles around yourself - there are reports that suggest it could help you stay safe. Certainly, a bullet made of silver will not be useful to you since it is believed that the Chindi has a spiritual nature, and therefore invulnerable to weapons.

The WOLF LEGENDS OF THE Quileute TRIBE

The Quileute tribe was sucked from the depths of obscurity into international celebrity thanks to the film and book franchise Twilight that depicted them as shapeshifters with lycanthropy who are the arch-enemies of vampires. The creator of the first novel, Stephenie Meyer, developed an urban legend of the Quileute tribe that has since been incorporated into mythology and urban mythology. In her tale the Quileute can transform into werewolves and fight vampires. The principal Quileute protagonist in the story, Jacob Black, has been a hero of a certain kind and the fascination with the Quileute has increased due to. While there isn't a myth of a shape-shifting Quileute culture It is believed that the Quileute are a close kinship with wolves. They also believe that their ancestors originated from wolves to human beings.

The Quileute myth of creation explains that the legendary Native American transformer Q'wati (sometimes called Dokibatt) traveled to their land and discovered that there were no living people. He first dipped his hands in a lake and then massaged them so that the dead tissue between the palms became small balls. Then, he released the ball into the water and changed it into fish, so humans could be able to eat something. Then he observed two wolves, who transformed into human beings. They were they were the very early Quileute people. The tribe was given its name and said that they'd always be strong and brave because they are the wolves. Also, since he observed that wolves were always in pairs, with one male , and one female decided that the Quileute men could only have one wife for each (though this did not apply to chiefs).

Q'wati also taught Quileute how to fish and hunt as well as he is featured in the myths of creation of other Native American tribes too, always as a protector and ally to humanity. The Quileute honor him, as well as their ancestors, by performing the 'wolf dance' which is performed by wearing a wolf mask that is carved out of cedar wood. Celebrations featuring the wolf dance continue to be held on their 1 square mile reservation in La Push, Washington (on the Pacific coast) until today. The preservation of the tradition is particularly crucial to the Quileute because they are of the belief that their sole brothers that are part of the Chimakum tribe were wiped out by the flood. They are therefore the most wolf-like of their kind.

While their main business was fishing, in recent times the Quileute have been exploring tourism as a way in order to generate revenue most of which comes from those who love The Twilight show, which come to the reservations from all over the world to discover what is behind shape-shifting wolves Meyer invented. The true legends of the Quileute tell of an ogress who devours children, as well as a massive wild man who captures fish using his razor-sharp nails However, the only shapeshifter they are convinced of is the trickster-like figure of the Raven and his tales tend to be comical rather than frightening. However, the old tale that the Quileute were created from wolves, combined with the contemporary tale that the Quileute may be able to transform back into its original shape, has proven to be one that has caught the imagination of many. The Quileute have come up with a method to make use of this modern mythology to ensure that their traditions are preserved for the next generation.

SKIDI PAWNEE

It is believed that the Skidi Pawnee are so closely linked to the wolves that they're often known as the Wolf Pawnee. A significant Pawnee myth of creation tells us that a meeting of all animals was at one point held on the sky however, The Wolf Star was not invited. Resenting this The Wolf Star sent down a grey wolf to follow the Storm That Comes From The West The Storm was responsible for caring for all creatures on the earth. The Storm carried an entire bag that included all the human beings in the world. When he came across a suitable location to hunt buffalo He would then release the bag's contents.

MINIDLESS RAGE

The Wolf did not come out till The Storm was asleep and then snatched the bag, believing it could be a food source. After the wolf had was able to open the bag, all humans rushed out. When they realized that there was no buffalo left to hunt, they became furious with the animal. In a rage of rage, they killed the wolf. Then, in the course of time, The Storm found them, and was able to see the act of murder they'd committed. He informed them that they had introduced death into this world, for the very first time and that it would be in their hearts for the rest of time. The Storm instructed the group to create an animal-shaped bag using the skin of a wolf, and then fill it with items that could remind them of the horrific crime they'd committed. From the moment they left, The Storm told them that they would be known as the Skidi also known as the Wolf Pawnee.

For the earliest colonists The Skidi Pawnee were known as a war-like tribe that protected their sacred lands with determination. They linked the constellations of stars with animals and also held ceremonies to make sure that spirits were content. The most well-known ceremonies was the 'Morning star Ceremony', during the ceremony, a young girl was sacrificed. This ritual was performed when a member of the tribe dreamed of it was the Morning Star required a sacrifice. It was then the tribe's turn to seize the young girl of another tribe to commit her to sacrifice by shooting an arrow into her heart. The last sacrifice was in 1848. A girl named Haxti who was 14 years old suffered the fate of being the victim.

THE WENDIGO

Though it has been more closely linked to the myth of the werewolf The Wendigo (sometimes known as Windigo) from Native American legend is quite distinct from the other creature, and is better described as an anthropomorphic creature. It is believed that the Algonquian people believe humans could be possessed by the Wendigo as well as those who commit cannibalism are more likely to be victims. Some versions of the myth claim that humans are transformed into Wendigos just through eating human flesh rather than being controlled by the spirit. Others suggest that greedyness is sufficient to transform a person to the form of a Wendigo. The transformation typically occurs in winter, and there are numerous reports claiming that the Wendigo could transform back to a human during spring.

The desire for HUMAN FLESH

When the transformation happens the half-human being that emerges is believed to be aggressive and gluttonous, and has an insatiable appetite of human flesh. The Wendigo appears like a recently dismembered human body, in a state of emaciation, bloody and partially decomposed with a ash-grey appearance and a strong smell that is a stench of flesh. The Wendigo's desire for human beings will never be satisfied as each feeding it becomes bigger, and thus requires more food to support its own needs. This is why it is always hungry, and in close proximity to starvation, regardless of the frequency at which it consumes. To take out a Wendigo and end its feeding frenzy it is necessary to burn its body, and then scatter the remains.

The confusion among werewolves and the Wendigo and werewolves may originate from reports of wolf-like animals being observed located in Wisconsin and Michigan. North American states of Wisconsin and Michigan roughly in the same region that the Wendigo is said to be found in. The "Bray Road Beast" as well as the "Michigan Dogman" are both thought to be wolf-like but possessing human characteristics like having two legs. It's not surprising that reports of werewolf-like creatures have been linked to the ancient stories of evil spirits in the same region, but in reality, the Wendigo is much more similar in appearance and behavior to an actual zombie than to the werewolf.

THE NAGUAL

Nagual (sometimes Nahual) of Mexico. Nagual (sometimes Nahual) of Mexico is a sorcerer with special affinities with an animal spirit (or Tonal). The mythology is believed to predate even the arrival of Europeans and, therefore, could be different from the earlier European stories of werewolves. It is believed that the

Nagual as well as his (or his or her) animal companions are spiritually bound throughout their lives, and live in and out of death together. In the night, the human is able to change into his animal companion , so that they are one. Any injury inflicted to the animal during the time it is controlled by Nagual Nagual will show up on the body of the human Nagual after he returns by way of example.

The connection between a person and an animal was established during the birth, based on the date on which the individual was born. If a person was born on a day that is associated with wolves as an example, could have a special connection with the wolf. The most commonly used forms picked by Naguals are bats, owls jaguars, pumas, and jaguars however, in theory, the case of a Nagual could transform into any animal.

Many stories speak of Nagual feeding on sleepy children Some Mexican parents put mirrors on their beds for this reason. The reflection of their child is believed to deter the Nagual. There are also stories about that of the Nagual taking blood from the child and causing illness. Some believe that Naguals are not able to cause disease. Nagual can't directly harm human beings and the Nagual seems to have been a respected part of certain communities. They were regarded as a palatable and nourishing by the society of their host in order to shield themselves from other spirits that were evil or hostile Naguals.

THE IJIRAAT

The Inuit shapeshifter can assume many forms, however it it most times, it is disguised as an wolf, with its bright red eyes revealing its true identity. Most people whom claim to have witnessed the Ijiraat claim that they saw this from the corner their eyes, briefly because the Ijiraat disappeared out of sight. The Ijiraat prefer species which are adept at moving quickly across the Arctic landscape. This could be the reason they are often observed as wolves. Bears and raccoons are of the other popular species.

There are a variety of opinions on how dangerous the Ijiraat may be for humans. Some claim they are frequently attacked particularly children, however some believe they're just messengers, or lost souls. According to one version the Ijiraat were believed to represent Inuit people who traveled too far North and ended up stuck between the land of people who are alive and graveyard of the deceased. One thing that the majority of accounts concur on is that any person who meets the Ijiraat quickly forget all memories of the incident.

QISARUATSIAQ

Qisaruatsiaq is known as an Inuit woman who was said to have was exiled from her community and became an Wolf. Qisaruatisaq was described as being a stubborn , lonely individual who would insist on building her own ice dwelling instead of sharing it with others in the people. She would go fishing on her own and return empty handed which she would then take from her neighbors. A few days ago, the Qiasaruatsiaq didn't not come back after one of her fishing excursions, and an individual tracker was sent out to locate her. Tracking her snowy footprints in the inland, he traveled for miles, before he noticed an area of one her tracks was transformed into the footprint of a clawed wolf. The tracks of the half-human and half-wolf disappeared in the distance and the tracker figured it was better to return.

Following this, many people have reported seeing Qisaruatsiaq's new wolf-like form while they went on hunts for caribou. They believe she became more and more wild until she eventually transformed into an untamed wild wolf. Within Greenland it is believed that there was a similar tale one of the Qivittoq which is described as a spirit who wanders who, after having left his village, grows the fur and claws of his prey until becoming more animal-like than human. The Qivittoq is said to periodically return to his community to take food items.

THE AMAROK

The Amarok is believed to be a huge creature resembling a wolf in the Arctic and that hunts on its own. There is speculation that the myth of the Amarok may be from the time of huge wolves actually lived alongside humans with the now extinct dire wolf being mentioned as a possible explanation for the legend. This wolf, known as the dire, was bigger than the current grey wolf and may be known to Inuit's ancestral ancestors who died in the midst of 10.000 years back. There isn't any evidence of any human-like behavior from the Amarok It is said to be a powerful animal that resembles a wolf, which is about one-third the height of mature man.

Amarok's description Amarok has many similarities to the mythical giant wolf, called the Waheela. The legend says that the wolf lives in the Northwest regions of Canada and hunt in small groups of three or two.

Hounds of God

Werewolves are usually viewed as being evil agents and often in alliance with Satan in their brutalization of innocent people. It is sometimes said that people change their appearance in their own desires. They were given the name binomial melancholia canina during the 10th century. Later in the 14th century they were referred to as daemonium lupum.

In 1692 at the time in the town of Jurgensberg in Livonia In 1692, a man of old age said that werewolves were not bad. He declared himself to be one, which was a extremely dangerous statement to make in a time when the punishment for being one was usually to be burned on the spot or more severe. Thiess The man, as he was known, declared that werewolves were in fact being benevolent creatures created by God and gave them the name of 'Hounds of God'. He claimed it was because the Hounds of God utilized their werewolf abilities to safeguard individuals. They Hounds of God were able to fight witches and demons in the deepest hell, keeping them from ascending into the heavens and inflicting havoc on women and men. Poor crops, he said was caused by the werewolves' inability to control evil spirits. Thiess insisted that, even being werewolf, he would still be in heaven. Unfortunately the judges who heard Thiess's arguments did not share his beliefs, however, they decided to not take the full weight of the law on him, limiting his sentence to ten lances.

THE BENANDANTI

There is a legend that states it was believed that old Thiess was one that was of the Benandanti kind. Benandanti were Benandanti were a specific kind of werewolf which did what Thiess claimed, fighting demons and evil spirits in the underworld known by the name of Malandanti. Their fights against the Malandanti took place during the four nights throughout the calendar year. and coincided with the times when crops were harvested or planted.

The Benandanti were always against witchcraft of any kind however in 1610, a small collection of Benandanti werewolves were brought to the Inquisition which was the Catholic Church's effort to weed out infringers and heretics against the canon of the Church. The Benandanti were accused of being guilty of witchcraft, and also of being witches. The Benandanti later turned into what they'd always foughtas evil werewolves. However, there are some indications that they'd lost the battle with Malandanti and it was actually witches from the underworld that were portrayed in the days before the Inquisition.

Werewolf Panic

The day that the German pastor and professor of theology Martin Luther, pinned his Ninety-Five Theses upon the front door of the Castle Church in Wittenberg on 31 October 1517, which sparked the Reformation The very existence of the Catholic Church was threatened. It took on the task of protecting its own by every means it could. One of them was a war on terror in the countries that remained which were loyal to Pope Francis in Rome in an effort to cleanse the population of the satanic practices and beliefs.

WEREWOLF TRIALS

While, in the past St Augustine as well as St Thomas Aquinas had criticized the lycanthropy belief, at the time of the 13th century the Church concluded the it was within their best interest to believe Satan was capable of making people werewolves or giving people the ability to transform themselves. Because the campaign from 1521 to 1600, a large number of people were tried for therianthropy and were transformed into wild animal. The first formal execution for werewolfism took place within Switzerland in 1407, when several defendants were beaten and burned to death at stake. However, with the Church's emphasis on reform, a greater quantity of trials were brought before courts. There was a lack of patience in these cases, and inquisitors – who were appointed by the Church to hunt down the heretics and Satanists are said to have dismembered suspects to locate the hair of wolves that was incriminating inside their bodies. In the event that there was no evidence discovered, the person accused was innocent. However, the person accused was also dead.

INWARD GROWING HAIR

The sad tale is told by one man of in the Lombard town Pavia who slayed a group of people in 1541 and attacked them as an animal. He was eventually arrested, however, he reassured the officers who restraining them that his only distinction from wolves was when a real wolf was killed, hair was sported outwards however, with him, it was growing into the inside. Naturally the magistrates wanted to prove this. Therefore, they took off his legs and arms in order to examine his internal organs. Naturally, there was nothing suspicious however, the man obviously, passed away. He was suffering from nothing more than illusions. But, it's worth mentioning that the notion of skin growing towards the inward direction is not a new concept. Versipellis also known as'skin-turning' is mentioned in a variety of old sources such as Petronius, Lucilius and Plautus It is also believed to be closely related to the older Norse word meaning the shapeshifter or werewolf Hamrammr.

THE PANIC SPREADS

In the same period as mentioned above was happening, there were said be plenty of werewolves in the region around the town of Constantinople (modern-day Istanbul) that the city's ruler sent troops into the countryside and took them on, killing around 150, according to reports. approximately 150. The 16th century French jurist Jean Bodin told the story of the Procurator General who claimed to have shot an arrow through the leg of a wolf. He also claimed the following day, a man was said to have been discovered in the bed with an arrow stuck within his hip. Bodin also referenced a treatise on sorcerers written by Pierre Marner in which the author claims to have witnessed people transformed into wolves in Savoy. Another account from that time relates the woodcutting peasant who was bitten by an wolf in a village close to Lucerne within Switzerland. He was able to defend himself by cutting off one animal's legs, at which point it changed into a woman and a woman who was missing an arm. She was burned alive. Many crimes were at the time blamed on demons or the devil who according to legend, allowed the criminal acts to be carried out when the culprit is disguised as an animal. Others were believed to be cursed by the desire to be an animal, and were also prone to eat flesh and drink the blood of their victims.

AUTHORITIES WARNINGS

The authorities who governed the countryside of France issued proclamations to warn citizens to be aware of the dangers of werewolves , as well as giving directions on how they could capture and punish the creatures if they were found to be in the outside world. They viewed shapeshifters as citizens living dangerous lives, putting others at risk by their actions. The demands of the authorities did not always work However, they were successful. In rural parts of France spiritual and mystical practices actually flourished , rather than decline. The practice of shapeshifting was viewed to many people as a blessing , not an affliction. Naturally, having a deal with the devil was also a reason to excuse many bad conduct from a lot of individuals, particularly those who had an intense sex urge.

The chance was frequently seized to falsely blame people for who a grudge was kept or against who the accused was engaged in a dispute of a nature. In this way, it was similar to those witchcraft trials that took place in England. In these chilly times it was fairly easy to concoct a convincing testimony and get someone to be convicted. The witnesses were seldom or never confronted with a particular interrogation, and the judge was often biased towards the evidence they perceived to be an untrustworthy, devious and fraudulent accused. In the event that the person accused of the crime was famous or famous individual, there was a bit of possibility of being dismissed as falsehood or hyperbole. If, however, the accused was an ordinary citizen or tortured or other method is always likely to result in the confession.

PIERRE BURGOT and MICHAEL VERDUN

The transformations of werewolves never took place in the courtroom or in front of impartial witnesses. They took place in remote areas as well as in the presence frequently, of witnesses who were not trustworthy. Yet there were reports of France about 30000 cases of 'infection' by werewolves was documented. One of the first and most famous trials for werewolves occurred in 1521. Pierre Burgot and Michel Verdun were tried in front of to the Domincans before the Domincans at Poligny in the Diocese of Alencon.

Burgot said to the court that 19 years ago while taking care of his sheep the day before, there was a massive storm that caused them to be scattered across the country. He was attempting to bring them back once more when three black horses arrived on the scene. After he had explained the situation one of the horsemen advised him to not worry because his master would take care of the horses for him. All he needed to do was to swear loyalty to this master. They agreed to come back in a couple of days. Burgot went on his way, thrilled soon after, to see his followers huddled together. When he came across the mysterious stranger after a couple of days when he was in court that he had discovered that his master was in reality the Satan. Burgot was willing to leave God or Christianity and join with Satan. In the following two years, he stopped going to church, that he did well and did not have any issues with his flock and church members, he returned to his attendance. But, at the time an individual identified as Michel Verdun brought him back to the fold of the devil, giving him money.

THE TRANSFORMATION

He was a part of a witches' s Sabbath where he was smeared by a salve, which changed him into an Wolf. He was extremely robust in this appearance and was able to move like a breeze. Afterward an additional salve was administered and he reverted to his human appearance. In the following years when he was a wolf, he took on a variety of adventures in the form of a wolf. These were expeditions in which he revealed to the court that he had been so fatigued that he was in bed for several days. He told of an attack against a boy who was between 6 and 7 years old, who screamed so loudly that he needed to quickly recover his human form to avoid being noticed. In another incident, a four-year old little girl became the target. The entire girl, aside of the arm that was eaten and the body was described by Burgot as excellent. Another girl was strangled , and her blood was drained. only a portion of her stomach was eaten by another. The bloodlust of the wolves grew so strong that they couldn't stop murdering. Much to the astonishment of the friars, they acknowledged having sexual relationships between female wolves. Naturally, the evidence was persuasive. Two suspects had been found guilty for witchcraft and were summarily executed.

The same time an individual hunter was said to have killed an Wolf with his sword, and then been following its bloody trail throughout the forest where he come across it. The trail eventually led to the hut, which was small. However, when he smashed in with the intention of killing this beast found the peasant Michel Udon, with a wound being bathed by an woman who was probably his wife. The peasant was detained and executed, along with two other people, Philibert Montot and another named as Gros Pierre who confessed with him, most likely after a time in the dungeon.

JACQUES ROLLET

The year was 1598. Jacques Rollet was accused of murder after two hunters came upon two wolves grazing on an unidentified 15 year old boy. The wolves fled after being interrupted, but the hunters, who were

Armed, pursued them. However, they then claimed, when they pursued them that the paw prints gradually changed into the human ones. They eventually tracked down and rescued their target who was an imposing, gaunt man with long hair that was matted and a long beard covered in dirty rags which were smashed on his body. They saw that his hands were swathed with blood, and what looked like human flesh was trapped in those long, long nails.

He explained to them that the name of his son was Jacques Rollet and confessed on the spot that he was possessing an ointment, which after he applied it onto his body changed him into an Wolf. He confessed that, as a wolf was viciously attacked by children and ate them, but claimed that he only did it because he struggling and his entire family in dire need of food. Incredibly, even though he was condemned to death however, the verdict was thrown out by the Parlement of Paris on the argument the fact that his brain was disordered and the judge was not able to plead. Instead of being executed his sentence was to be confined to an infirmary for the remainder all of his time. This could be the beginning of the belief that the behavior of the wolf might be explained by medical causes instead of supernatural reasons.

ILLICIT RELATIONS WITH DEMONS

In the midst of all this panic Women were not spared from being viewed as suspects. Francois Secretain , who was executed following she admitted to participating in rituals where other women , animals and children were killed , and also for being involved in illicit relationships with the demon. The method was the same every time but with a different name. A child or a woman might be discovered, possibly attacked by wild animals. The sightings of wolves within the area were brought to the authorities' attention. They would then arrest suspects and confessions would eventually follow the horrific treatment they were made to endure. Trials and the inevitable execution followed.

The real reason for the many deaths of victims in these cases was evidently, they may have been killed and eaten by actual wolves. It is also possible that the communities, engulfed by the fear of being hysterical and fear of being a victim, were required to find reasons to blame the victims and the executions of these scapegoats could rid them of the evil they thought that was lurking in their midst.

In 1603, more than 600 people believed to be shapeshifters had been burned to death as well as there were no limits in sight to the executions and trials over the years despite opposition growing in the voice of powerful people.

Chapter 7: Freud's Wolf Man

The Wolf Man, whose real name was Sergei Pankejeff, was one of the most well-known patients of Dr. Sigmund Freud. He was the eminent pioneer of psychoanalysis. Pankejeff was a troubled Russian nobleman who sought treatment under Dr. Freud in the year 1910.

After a lengthy period of study, Freud published his history of the case. He named his patient "The Wolf Man' to protect his identity and because he believed that Pankejeff's frequent dream, where the patient saw a group of wolves sat in the branches of a tree, was important. The case would become a ground-breaking event in the field of psychoanalysis. within the case, Freud asserted the significance of early experiences for the development that the adult brain develops and specifically emphasized sexual awakening in the infant which was a novel idea in the moment he began writing.

Sergei Pankejeff came from a wealthy St Petersburg family, and was educated having studied in Russia as well as Germany. But the family was plagued by an underlying mental disorder and this was made worse by the political turmoil that was sweeping Russia in the era. Sergei's elder sister Anna who was bipolar committed suicide in the year 1906. In the following year his father Konstantin also committed suicide. Sergei who was located in Munich when the death of his father suffered from depression for a long time and sought the help of several psychiatrists in order to treat his depression.

TWO SUCICIDES

In 1910, his personal doctor took him to Vienna to see Dr. Sigmund Freud. The doctor was making a name of himself as a neurologist who specialized in psychosomatic diseases. Alongside the depression, Pankejeff was suffering from numerous physical ailments, including constipation that was chronic (he could only get through a movement by using an enema) and blurred vision (he believed his eyes were looking at his surroundings through a fog-like cover). He could not take care of himself and was dependent on many caregivers.

Despite his suffering and desperate need for help, Freud found his new patient extremely passive. His approach was that of apathy, and he was incredibly intolerant of examination.

Contrary to Freud's norms and stance, he set Pankejeff an estimated time of one year to complete his therapy in the hope that it will motivate him to continue. The time frame, Freud believed, helped Pankejeff cooperate in the therapy.

SIX White SEVEN WOLVES

In the year 1899, Freud released his work The Interpretation of Dreams, proposing his theory that the seemingly chaotic material that we recall from our dreams can actually be very significant and can provide a glimpse into the motivations and desires of our subconscious mind. The desires that we experience, Freud claimed, are predominantly sexual in nature, and are hard to comprehend, as society requires us to suppress these desires in our daily lives. In this way, Freud concentrated his treatment for Pankejeff in relation to a frequent dream which had troubled him since early childhood. By paying attention to the exact words as well as the narrative and images his patient employed, Freud recounted Pankejeff's dream in the following manner:

I woke up dreaming that it was night and I was in the bed ... When I woke up, the window opened on it's own volition and I was frightened to discover that a group of white wolves had gathered on the large walnut tree that was in the windows. There were at least six or seven. The wolves were white and appeared like sheepdogs or foxes ... With complete fear, and evidently consumed by the beasts, I yelled at them and fell asleep. My nurse was quick to get me to my room to find out what was happening to me. The process took a period of time before I realized that it was an illusion; I saw an incredibly clear and vivid image of the window opening and the wolves perched at the foot of the tree.

In addition to telling the story of the dream, Pankejeff sketched a picture of wolves in the tree. It was odd that the wolves were just five on his drawing, instead of the seven or six that the dreamer had described in his description of his dream.

THE PRIMAL SCENE

Freud's interpretation of this dream which was extremely unusual it suggested that the animals were the patient's father and that the dream was a result of an unrecollection that the child had experienced that he witnessed his parents arguing. Freud believed that it was likely the child entered the bedroom of his parents and witnessed the two of them having sex, and the father grabbing his mother away from behind. A misinterpretation of the scene that led to the fear of castingration and a primitive desire for sexual intimacy toward his father, led to the child's sexuality and sexuality to change and a profound neurosis was born that lasted throughout adulthood. Because of this, Freud made the notes of The Wolf Man case, from the history of an infantile Neurosis.

According to Freud's story the extended treatment he received from The Wolf Man proved beneficial and as a consequence Pankejeff was relieved from several of his most troublesome symptoms. He would later become one of Freud's famous patients, and was also one of the best examples of the positive results of psychoanalysis. Many times, he was mentioned by Freud as evidence of the effectiveness of the "talking cure", Pankejeff later came out in the form of The Wolf Man and also worked with Freudian psychoanalysts till his death in 1979.

Succeed or fail?

There were opponents of Freud who claimed that the treatment given to The Wolf Man was by far not as successful as was claimed. Witnesses reported that a couple of years after the treatment, Pankejeff was seen in on the street of Vienna gazing in the mirror, with the impression of a physician having made through his nose. It's no surprise that there was some doubt as to how effective the "talking cure" had been in the case. Other people, for instance, Austrian journalist Karin Obholzer, who interviewed Pankejeff during the 1970s, said the fact that The Wolf Man himself did not believe in the conclusion Freud came to when he analyzed the dream. Pankejeff stated that he didn't have any memories of witnessing his parents couling in the dream, and it was extremely unlikely that he could ever witness such an incident. In the most affluent Russian families, youngsters would not have been able to barge at their parents this manner. They would have been sleeping in their bedrooms with their nannies He said that they wouldn't have seen their parents engaging in sexual activities or asked them for help when they awoke at night.

FAMILY TRAUMA

At first, Pankejeff said that he had believed Freud's theory, and thought he would wait for his childhood memory to surface but it didn't. Through many years, he come to the conclusion that Freud was wrong in diagnosing him and that the root of his condition had not in connection with the experience of the reminiscence of a sexual encounter between his parents when they were young and was more about his traumatic relationship with his deceased sister. In fact, it seems plausible, on the face of it that the suicides within the immediate Pankejeff family the sister's as well as his father's be more troubling to Pankejeff than a memories of sexual activity from childhood. childhood.

The Wolf Man case was later revised through psychologists Maria Torok and Nicolas Abraham in their book, The Wolf Man's Secret Word In the book, they demonstrate how the multilingual background of Pankejeff's could have had an impact on the contents of his dreams. They argue that Russian word for sister,'siestorka" is very similar in meaning to Russian phrase "pack of six "shiestorka," and, by using a new concept they call "cryptonymy," they found that, rather than being about his relationship with his family, the animals might be a symbol of his sister and his wish to have his sister's back and watch over his.

FREUD'S LEGAL

In the following years, the Wolf Man case was discussed by philosophers Gilles Deleuze and Felix Guattari who believed Freud's stance on the causality of sexuality in all neurosis was simplistic, and that he was too simplistic in his thought. They also presented evidence to prove that Pankejeff was on and off of treatment for years following his meetings with Freud and believed that his research to have been a failure. It is now like Freud overstated the effectiveness in The Wolf Man case, and his emphasis on the significance of the scene that Pankejeff claimed to have witnessed was incorrect. But, it can't be denied that certain aspects of the study were groundbreaking as well as when studying the

the cause of neurosis during the early years of childhood, Freud showed great insight. He was adamant about listening to what patients had to say to him and taking note of psychic information like dreams, that was previously overlooked when treating mental illnesses was also revolutionary and fundamentally humane in the way it was approached.

The famous analysis of Freud of The Wolf Man, despite its numerous flaws is still one of the most important psychoanalysis texts, and continues to spark debate and controversy with regard to its containing the most significant Freud's theories on the universality of infantile sexuality, castingration anxiety and The Oedipus complex, the repression and the distinction of the mind between the ego, id, and superego.

This is the Full Moon Killer

It was 1985, and 32 people had perished in Florence over the last 17 years, with the majority of them being killed in nighttime when the moon was full. These were mostly lovers, killed and mutilated in the cars that were parked on streets with no one. They were shot through the car's windows, and a sharp instrument that was believed of being a scalpel was used to cut their bodies after death, with sexual organs, or breasts, often being removed.

DOUBLE MURDER

The incident began in the month of August, 1968, when an unidentified man and his lover were killed near a cemetery within the suburban area of Florence. The girl was married, and her husband, who was jealous, was immediately investigated. He was detained and confessed. He was found guilty for the two murders, the man was sentenced to jail. Then, shortly after he retracted his plea, however nobody believed the story. He was arrested in the end, and he left his home the following day the murders, carrying a bag. The case appeared to be closed and six years later, on September 14, 1974, another murder in Florence. A couple, who were in their vehicle in a street that was deserted were killed and disfigured with the woman being attacked 96 times. The .22 bullets that were fired from the Berreta pistol, were identical to those used to kill the couple in the year 1968.

The MONSTER OF FLORENCE

Seven years passed until the incident that followed on June 6, 1981. The couple was killed in their vehicle as the female's sexual organs had been mutilated. The police began calling the murderer the 'Monster from

Florence'. A couple who was gay were killed in 1983 by the same Berreta that was used in the earlier murders. No mutilation was evident involved in the case, and investigators considered whether the killer been mistaken, believing the victims inside the vehicle to be the couple who were courting. After the final murders in 1985 the prosecutor's assistant received an envelope with strips of fleshthat had been cut from the breast of the final woman murdered.

A SUBSPECT IS IDENTIFIED

The investigation had been thorough in the 17 years that followed the initial murders, and more than 100,000 were questioned regarding the case. It was only in early 1990s when suspicion started to befall an 68-year-old farmer Pietro Pacciani, whose hobby was taxidermy. He was already serving jail time for beating and stamping a man death, and was also known to have sexually assaulted his daughters. Incredibly, however, Pacciani was also a part of an occult organization. Pacciani was adamant about his innocence throughout his trial, and evidence against him proved not strong however, he was found guilty of murder in seven cases. He was released upon appeal two of his co-conspirators, Mario Vanni and Giancarlo Lotti, were both arrested and found guilty of their role in five murders.

While the public and media believed in the guilt of Pacciani, Pacciani was granted a second trial, however, before the case could be brought back to the court, he passed away of a poisoning. The fact that these crimes were carried out under the full moon, and in a state of a frenzy with Pacciani's fascination with the occult, has convinced many that werewolf-like traits were in some level, however the truth of it all died with him.

Albert Fish

"The Werewolf of Wysteria

A sadist, paedophile and a killer of cannibals who has horrible bestial tendencies, Albert Fish has been declared by experts as the most insane human being to ever. In a police interview, Fish explained that he changed uncontrollably through a 'blood thirst that was brewing within me'. After the transformation was over Fish was deeply upset.

"I would have offered my life in less than a minute of doing this to bring back her life', he stated.

A violent character metamorphosis, that is followed by unremitting remorse, are common signs of classic psychosis of the werewolf. Albert Fish showed all the obvious signs of being the most powerful Lycan.

THE BURNING WOLF Within

Also known as the Werewolf of Wysteria, the Grey Man, the Brooklyn Vampire and The Boogeyman, Albert Fish was an American serial killer and cannibal. Fish claimed that he ate and molested children from all over in the United States. Even though Fish was believed to be responsible for at least 15 murders Fish eventually admitted to three. Fish claimed to have committed more than more than 100 crimes against young children. The werewolf-like anger within him was unleashed this innocent, gray-haired man turned into a terrifying flesh-tearing creature.

He was a lover of inflicting pain, and inflicting pain on himself. He put needles in his body, particularly in the the perineum and groin; following his arrest and discovery of twenty-nine needles by X-ray. He put alcohol-coated balls of cotton wool inside the anus of his body. He would then light the balls to purify himself from his transgressions'. He committed the same horrific crimes and did even more to the victims of his children. In his trial, the jury took just under an hour to come to the verdict of guilty. Fish expressed his gratitude to the judge for his death sentence through electrocution. An Daily News reporter wrote, his eyes were sparkling with joy at the thought of being smothered by a scorching heat that was more intense than the fires with which Fish would often smear his flesh to satisfy his cravings.'

On the 16th of January, 1936 Albert Fish was executed in the Sing Sing maximum security prison in New York state, he was shackled into "Old Sparky the electric chair after which, just three minutes later, he was dead. The report says that he declared that electrocution would be the most thrilling experience that I have ever experienced'.

CHILDRHOOD WHIPPINGS

Albert Fish was born Hamilton Fish in 1870. His father, who was aged 43 years old that his mother. When his father passed away in

1875, the young Hamilton was enrolled in St John's Orphanage by his mother. There Hamilton changed his name to Albert to be free of the nickname "Ham and Fish which was given to him by other children.

The orphanage life was harsh and brutal. There were frequent beatings and whippings. However paradoxically, Albert grew to enjoy the suffering. He was so enthralled in fact that he'd even get erections that the others in the class mocked the other children. The mother of the child was in a position help him once more when she got a job in 1879, however Albert had already been scarred from his experience during his time at St John's. When he was 12 he was involved in a sexual relationship. His Telegraph boy was the one who introduced him to sinister behaviors like coprophagia or drinking urine. He would spend his weekends watching boys stripping in public baths.

MALE PROSTITUTE

Fish said that in 1890 the time he began employed as an adult prostitute within New York City and that the young men he raped were frequently. In 1898, he was became a father and married, and had six children. He was an artist for painting houses, but also was molesting numerous children, mostly minors who were younger than. Then Fish began to show an interest in the practice of castration. He decided to try it with a man Fish had been in an affair; however, the man left before Fish could execute the experiment.

Fish's life was completely changed in 1917 after his wife went off with a man. Fish began to act more bizarrely than before. Fish claims to have heard voices. He even wrapped himself in the carpet, telling people that he was ordered to do this from St John. The children of his reported that he beating himself on his naked body using a nail-studded piece from wood, until it was covered in blood. They witnessed him standing alone on a hill, his hands raised and shouting "I Christ. Christ.'

THE Wolf IN THE Woods

In 1924, seven year old Francis McDonnell was playing with others near his house at Staten Island. His mother noticed an unruly man. He walked around the street, shaking his hands , and pretending to talk. She walked away from the man and walked back inside. That same day, the man took Francis into a nearby forest. The next day , his body was discovered sexually battered, mauled and strangled. It would take another 10 years before the police could discover that the murderer is Albert Fish.

The year was 1927. Fish took Billy Gaffney. He tortured him and then murdered him during a wild panic. Fish later recounted the tale with great enthusiasm:

I whipped his naked tummy until the blood dripped from his legs. I cut off his nose, ears, and cut his mouth from ear to. I slit his eyes and gouged them out. He was dead at that point. I put the knife in his stomach and I held my mouth against his body . I took a sip of his blood.

However, it was the murder of Grace Budd that led to Fish's eventual arrest. At the time Fish was age 58 He walked up to the Budds the Budds' doorstep in May 1928 pretended to be Frank Howard, a farmer from Farmingdale, New York. Fish was responding to an advertisement published on The New York World by Edward Budd Grace's 18-year-old brother, who was looking for work.

THE WOLF RETURNS

Fish told a story about how the farmer needed help on his farm, and Edward was keen to help. Fish returned after a couple of days and confirmed that Edward was hired and was invited to join him for lunch. There, Fish befriended Grace. Grace sat on his lap at the dining table. Much like the wolf from the tale about Little Red Riding Hood, Albert Fish decided to eat the girl. While he was about depart, he mentioned that the he was headed to a party for children at the house of his sister and was wondering if Grace would like to join with him. Grace's mother was not sure but her husband believed it was a good idea for the girl , and off Grace went along with Albert Fish. The last time they'd ever see of their daughter.

He took the unaware Grace to a train trip to the Bronx and later into the town that is Worthington within Westchester. To pay for Grace the ticket was an one-way ticket. Grace was fascinated by the forty-minute journey to the countryside. In her entire life, only twice has she been away from the city. It was a great reward for her. They took a walk along a road that was not well-known until they came across an abandoned two-story structure called Wysteria Cottage, which was situated in the middle of a forest. Fish was taken to the second floor and stripped off his clothes. He returned the scene

After she saw me completely naked, she began crying and attempted to climb down the staircase. I held her and she told me she was going to inform her mother. First , I stripped her naked. She did kick and bit and rub. I took her down then cut her into tiny pieces to carry my food to my room. Cook it and then consume it. What a sweet and soft tiny sexy limbs were when she was baked inside the oven. It took me nine days to finish eating her whole body.

A UNCONTROLLABLE BESTIAL RAGE

In the end, it Fish's arrogance was the reason he lied to Fish. Fish wrote a letter addressed to the mother of Grace six years after the fact in which he boasted about the murder. The letter was sent inside an envelope with its logo, which was that of New York Private Chauffeur's Benevolent Association. It was later discovered that a janitor from the group was left with some stationary at the boarding house after the time came to leave. Albert Fish had moved in following his departure. The detective William F. King waited at the residence and, when Fish arrived, he asked Fish to accompany him to the police headquarters in order to answer a few questions. Fish was threatening King with a razor however, the policeman was able to overpower the man and took him into custody.

Fish confessed to the killing of Grace Budd launching a debate about whether the unpredictable, violent rages that raged within him proved that he had no guilt, or possessed of an insanely divided personality. But, he was determined to be both rational and guilty, and sentenced to be executed. Following his sentence, he confessed that he had killed Francis McDonnell. Between 1924-1932 in addition to the three murders that could be attributed to his name as it is possible that the Werewolf of Wysteria may have killed many more children. In 1936 the electric chair in Sing Sing made sure that the wolf inside Albert Fish would hunt no further.

Chapter 8: Werewolves In Fiction

The genre of Werewolf Fiction is an intriguing and varied collection of works which is often heavily rooted into the rich long-standing mythology and folklore that surrounds the werewolf. It is depicted in a variety of media, including the horror literature of films, dramas, magazines games, television and music The stories that are told are, naturally typically supernatural tales that are designed to amuse and scare, but there are also symbolism and allegorical stories that are intended to inform or to warn people about certain actions.

Through time the portrayal of the werewolf evolved dramatically. In earlier times was the curse associated with being a werewolf typically viewed as a punishment for non-conformity, both in the eye of the ancient cultures as well as in the eyes early Christians. Stories of Saint Patrick changing Welsh King Vereticus to a werewolf in the wake of refusing to follow Christianity provide evidence of that.

Later, in the medieval era as the Catholic Church struggled against the rising growth of the Reformation The werewolves became feared creatures, allied with Satan, as a symbol of what would happen to those who did not follow the correct way. Through the twentieth century, movies have a depictions of werewolves were popular like Lon Chaney Jr.'s genre-defining film in 1941's film The Wolf Man, in where he's seen as a depressed, lonely outsider who accidentally became a werewolf, changed the public's perceptions. These days, werewolf-related characters are usually ones who are sympathetic, fighting evil or trying to lead a an ordinary life regardless of the obstacles they face when the moon is full.

In the past there were many tales of people who transformed into wolves. One of these stories is Homer's description of the Odyssey of the creatures the mysterious and beautiful Circe was enchanted to transform into were-lions and werewolves. Even Odysseus's people fell for her tricks and turned into were-swine. It was however in the middle ages of romances - the literary genre of heroics of chivalry that was popular in the aristocratic circles of High Medieval and Early Modern Europe The first time werewolves appeared. Up until around 1600 the fantastic stories about the exploits of princes, kings and knights, of damsels and dragons suffering - and sometimes, werewolves are hugely popular and the top-selling books of the day.

The romantic tales that follow Bisclavret as well as Guillaume de Palerme (see pages 64-5) portray the werewolf as a gentle creature as a victim of fate and a victim of evil magic and knights with evil intentions. Folklore tells us that the werewolf was far from harmless. Medieval theology has an influence on the depiction of this creature, naturally and religious men who wanted to be part of a people who were conscious of the dangers of going to the supernatural. The werewolf was depicted as a human who has erred and made a deal with Satan as a servant of his and performing his orders. The taboo on cannibalism, perhaps the most extreme among all - is shattered by these creatures, causing an intense hatred and disdain within the populace at large.

SEXUAL THEMES

From the very beginning sexual themes are typically found in the werewolf genre. In the movie Werewolf of London, the protagonist kills his lover out of jealousy for sexual pleasure when she walks with an ex-love. A film titled American Werewolf of London has a romance between David who is his fellow American named in the movie,, and an aspiring nurse named Alex whom is a love interest for him as well as Michael Jackson's Thriller video is set against the backdrop of the musician taking his girlfriend home, and putting a ring onto her finger to signify that they're going to be steady.

The story of Little Red Riding Hood (see page 132) is a classic filled of Freudian imagery and allegories. There are many levels of meaning in this story, ranging starting with the simple tale about the consequences for not following the things you're told to do to the symbolic meaning of living as represented by the rock which Little Red Riding Hood places within the wolf prior to sewing her back up. The novel by Angela Carter The Company of Wolves and the film Ginger Snaps, as well as a myriad of other fictional portrayals of werewolves, are owed an enormous amount to this fairy story.

GOTHIC HORRROR

The popularity of Gothic horror stories in the 19th century offered plenty of occasions for the werewolf myth to be revisited. A genre that combined romance and horror was created during 1764. Horace Walpole with his novel The Castle of Otranto and its mixture of melodrama as well as parody resulted in a delightful kind of terror. It was colored heavily with the Romantic literary style, which was relatively new at the time Walpole began writing. Werewolves were among the wonderful assortment of characters in the genre which included vampires, magicians, creatures (such as Frankenstein's Monster, invented in the work of Mary Shelley), demons as well as angels, dragons and.

G.W.M. Reynolds The 1847 Gothic novel Wagner the Wehr-Wolf, was an exemplary illustration of the genre. It is an account of the story of a German peasant who makes an agreement with Satan to transform into an infamous werewolf once every seven years for a better life. In the novel, main character Wagner depicts the positive and negative side of our personality The wolf's appearance demonstrates the dark and evil side we all have.

The 20th century was a time of countless werewolf novels, stories and movies. One of the experts in the genre was the legendary supernatural storyteller Algernon Blackwood, who included werewolves in several of his stories. Also, the rise of the comic book throughout the United States from the 1920s through the 1950s offered a different way to tell these stories particularly in titles such like Weird

Tales for which writers like H. Warner Munn, Seabury Quinn, and Manley Wade Wellman wrote incredibly horrifying stories.

It was in 1933 that American novelist, Guy Endore published The Werewolf of Paris, one of the novels that has been believed to be the werewolf equivalent of Bram Stoker's Dracula. Hammer Films produced an adaptation of the novel in the year 1961's The Curse of the Werewolf. In 1935, the film Werewolf of London added a fresh twist to the legend and was the first one to show an human-like werewolf. This gave an element of humanity into the animal, and also evoked an emotional response from the viewers. The werewolf also introduced to films the theme of the werewolf constantly murdering the thing he loved the most.

THE CLASSIC MOVIE WEREWOLF

The new werewolf style was made into an entire character we could have a conversation with Lon Chaney Jr.'s portrayal of the Wolf Man in Universal

Pictures 1941's release. The lycanthropy of the past was depicted in a completely negative light as a curse, or disease, and we felt completely for the suffering. Incredibly, the werewolf's personality however nice or kind he appears when he is in human form, remains treacherous, cruel and bloody when he goes through the painful - and it's always a painful and painful experience on film - transformation to the lupine form.

The most famous of films werewolves Lon Chaney, Jr. to reprise the role many times, and in his films certain elements of the standard werewolf mythology are well-established including that full moon-like transformation in Frankenstein Meets The Wolf Man of 1943 and silver bullets as the sole method of killing werewolves in the House of Frankenstein of 1944. He also played The Wolf Man in 1945's House of Dracula and in the comical Abbot and Costello Meet Frankenstein. After a short break, werewolf movies suddenly came to prominence again in 1981, with two massively popular films The Howling and

An American Werewolf in London. An American Werewolf in London and The Howling.

THE CONTEMPORARY BEAST

The modern-day werewolf has been associated with distinct from the portrayals from the past. Environmental issues have been cited as an emblem of a human being more attuned to the natural world. This role-playing adventure game Werewolf: The Apocalypse allows players to play the role of werewolves Garoux who are fighting the forces known as Gaia and fight against the destructing supernatural spirit known as the Wyrm which is a symbol of industrialization and pollution.

The popular Dr. Who and the Harry Potter books have both included werewolves. The latter of which depicts a professor, Remus Lupin, as an enraged werewolf, fearful of spreading his illness. The Harry Potter series, however while werewolves are depicted as threats however, they are also depicted as symbols of marginalized groups who were savagely abused or discriminated against. It is now commonplace to depict werewolves in fiction as distinct race or species. Sometimes, as well, people are depicted as having special powers or powers that permit them to change into werewolves at any time. In the fiction they are transformed into werewolves at birth or when victimized by werewolves.

Little Red Riding Hood

The fairy story of Little Red Riding Hood is perhaps the most well-known of werewolf tales. It is true that the character in the tale is usually described as the 'Big Bad' wolf. Big Bad' wolf, but it also is human-like, which tells us that this isn't a just a animal. The tale can be traced back to oral stories that were popular in various European nations, probably prior to in the seventeenth century. French peasants narrated the story in the 14th century , and it was also reported around the time of Italy in a variety of various versions.

Its conscious or unconsciously associated with werewolves is always present. Actually, a variant of the story called The Story of a Grandmother was published in 1870, though it's definitely older, refers to the antagonist in the tale as a bzou. This is a different name for wolf. The story is likely to reflect the hysteria about werewolves which was common in the medieval era. The full extent of the werewolf trials, like the ones of German serial killer Peter Stubbe, are illustrated in different versions of the tale in which the wolf eats the flesh of the grandmother to the child.

SEXUAL CONNOTATIONS

The first time it was published was through Charles Perrault in Paris in 1697. The sexual connotations that are often associated with the tale are evident in the illustrations accompanying the story. The illustration showed the wolf sleeping over the girl. French popular slang for a woman who shed her virginity, was "seen the wolf'. Another interpretation of the story is one of sexual awakening. the red cloak represents the menstrual cycle, while the dark forest symbolizes womanhood, and the wolf is a symbol of an individual who may be sexually seduced, a lover as well as a sexual predator.

The story was told, and retold over the decades in various mediums. It was adapted in 2011 for the big screen with the release of the American movie called Red Riding Hood. In this adaptation of the tale that was written by Twilight Director Catherine Hardwicke an isolated village is afflicted by the werewolf. The story is set in the middle ages , and is centered around Valerie (Amanda Seyfried) who is married to a wealthy gentleman named Henry (Jeremy Irons) however, she is in relationship with Peter (Shiloh Fernandez). The couple decide to flee away to be together. They are planning depart when they learn that the sister of Valerie was killed by the werewolf. The creature has been controlled by the people who offered each month a sacrifice of animals. However, this time and under the dark red lunar night, the waswolf been begging for human flesh. The villagers seek the aid from werewolf hunters Father Solomon (Gary Oldman) who brings along the realization that the werewolf can take on human form at night which causes the group to become distrustful of one another. As the panic grows, Valerie is determined to discover the identity of the beast making herself more vulnerable to danger.

In its most eloquent form, Little Red Riding Hood is easily one of the greatest stories about werewolves and is proven by its persistence through the ages and its hidden messages that continue to educate and entertain.

The Strange case of Dr Jekyll & Mr Hyde

Robert Louis Stevenson (1886)

The myth of the werewolf is obviously, frequently considered to be an analogy for the dual nature inherent in human beings, and the struggle which is waged in each one of us between the good and the evil. Charles Darwin theorized that, being apes that evolved into humans man, he has an animalistic side which is held in an intricate balance only with morality, and by the rigors of our modern-day society. In his novel of 1886, The Strange Case of Dr Jekyll and Mr Hyde, Robert Louis Stevenson explores the dual nature of us all with the characters of the title are symbols for the two human aspects.

The life of Dr Henry Jekyll is a battle against evil one that has resulted in him segregating himself from those who love his. The poison he concocts transforms Jekyll into a younger but brutal and unremorseful Mr. Edward Hyde who is the bad side of his character that is made manifest in a repulsively violent way as a murderer that is becoming difficult to manage. As Hyde becomes stronger Jekyll realizes that he's having difficulty remaining who he is.

The story begins on a Sunday morning, when a prominent London lawyer Gabriel

John Utterson and his acquaintance and distant cousin, Richard Enfield, take an excursion through London. Enfield shares with his companion the story of an unusual encounter he experienced recently. When he returned home late at evening, he witnessed unattractive-looking man stomping on the tiny screaming girl. As a crowd began to gather in the area, that man Hyde was seen escaping through a back door located in the back of a home that was owned by Jekyll and returned with PS100 to settle her family. The payment came by way of cheque that was signed by Jekyll.

UNSCIENTIFIC BALDERDASH'

Jekyll is actually an employee of Utterson and Utterson discovers that the doctor has made an estate plan that leaves the entirety of his wealth and possessions to Hyde. Confused, Utterson decides to investigate further by staking outside the Jekyll's residence, through which Hyde was able to find the money to pay for the girl's parents. After a long time Utterson is able to see Hyde come in through the door and begin a conversation with him. Hyde is now uneasy about Utterson's inquiries is rushing into the home. When he knocks on the front door, Utterson is told by Jekyll's butler Poole Poole, that Hyde is the only person who has access to the home. Incredulous, Utterson consults a friend who is also acquainted with Jekyll. Dr Hastie Lanyon explains to Utterson that he's been a bit irritable with Jekyll many years earlier due to an argument over Jekyll's research. It has been described by the doctor as unscientific balderdash. Then, some time after, Utterson has the opportunity to inquire about Jekyll himself regarding the mystery of Hyde after being asked to attend a meal celebration at his home. Jekyll is furious with the questioning of Utterson However, he simply affirms in a stern manner that Hyde will be his beneficiary in the event of his death.

One year later an elderly gentleman of repute known as Sir Danvers Carew, a member of the Parliament, is murdered .

Although the perpetrator has fled before being caught The maid has identified the victim as Hyde. When Utterson and police reach Hyde's residence and discover by the homekeeper Hyde has left. They immediately search for Jekyll who hands them an email from Hyde saying that he would disappear for ever. Jekyll, on the other hand, Jekyll insists that he would like nothing to have to do with him.

A MYSTERIOUS EVELOPE

Jekyll is seen to transform as she goes missing with Hyde and becomes more accessible and social. As a result, Lanyon dies suddenly, leaving behind an envelope to Utterson. The envelope is mysteriously sealed envelope, with instructions that it should not be opened until the disappearance or death of Jekyll. Utterson can't help but think that it may contain information regarding Hyde.

Utterson and Enfield still enjoy their usual Sunday morning constitutional. On one occasion, as they walk by Jekyll's home, they glance up and catch glimpses of him in the window. They invite him to join them for their walk, however, the doctor seems scared or suffering from severe pain and walks to the side. Utterson along with Enfield are both a bit upset by the incident.

In the next few minutes, Utterson receives a visit at his home by Jekyll's assistant, Poole who is concerned regarding his master. He informs Utterson that Jekyll is not leaving his lab over the last week, and that he had taken the scientist on numerous trips to scientists in a search for a drug that was not found. Poole was insistent on behalf of the legal team that Jekyll had been killed because the voice he heard inside the laboratory did not sound like that of his boss. The murderer, he argued is therefore in the lab. Utterson is willing to go back to the house along with the servant to look into the matter and when they arrive the two men take down the locked doors to the laboratory. In shock, they discover that the mysterious man Poole was referring to has committed suicide through poison consumption.

There is the corpse of Hyde wearing Jekyll's clothes. They go through the house looking for Jekyll but they find no trace of his body. However, they do discover a letter written to Utterson. The note instructs him to go back to his residence and read the letter inside the sealed envelope which has been given to Utterson by Lanyon. The letter turns out to be the "confession" of Jekyll.

Lanyon says that Jekyll wrote to him, asking him to follow his instructions. He was directed to go to the laboratory of Jekyll and search for the items listed in the letter. Then, he was instructed to bring them back to the house. Around midnight, someone Lanyon didn't know was expected to call the house to inquire about the items. As it turned out, Lanyon goes on, the person who was threatening come to the door at the hour of midnight, declaring that he was coming to retrieve the items Jekyll demanded Lanyon to take out of his lab. The man demanded an "graduated glass" and quickly pouring the powders and liquids into it. He then drank the resultant potion. Lanyon was shocked by the scene that unfolded before him The terrifying creature was beginning to change into his old friend, Jekyll. Lanyon concludes the letter by letting Utterson his friend who appeared at his doorstep at midnight was not a different person than Hyde.

A DOUBLE LIFE

In the second letter, Jekyll writes about how he been living a double existence and had committed a number of sins that he regretted. He decided to study the possibilities of science-based separation of his positive side from his dark side, and in his studies found a way to transform himself into a being who was free of the restrictions of conscience, Hyde. But, the second persona that he created was not good and, as a matter of fact his identity was not the ideal of goodness. He became worried when he realized he was changing into Hyde at will and determined to end his experiments. In the night, however his urge to commit suicide was stronger and he was able to kill the Sir Danvers Carew.

A FINAL ENDING to the madness

He writes that He resolved to end the changes, and he enrolled in charitable work which he believed would have redeemed him. However, the uncontrollable changes got more intense and he was finding himself needing the help of Lanyon in regaining the Jekyll self. The potion was beginning to run out, and it was becoming difficult to make any more because the key to this was an impurity that was present in the initial batch which he wouldn't be able to duplicate. In the face of having to live the life of Hyde and his plight, he decided to take his own life.

The Strange Case of Dr Jekyll and Mr Hyde stands with Bram Stoker's Dracula (1897) and Mary Shelley's Frankenstein as among the greatest masterpieces of Gothic horror. Its unending popularity can be seen, along with these works, in the multitude of adaptations, film stage, television, and stage that have been produced. The impact of the novel has been enormous with characters such like The Hulk, Two-Face and many other shape-shifting comic book superheroes.

Steppenwolf

Herman Hesse (1926)

In 1924, as he was living in Basel In 1924, in Basel, in 1924, the German author Herman Hesse left behind the issues of his union and moved to an apartment. In despair over his inability to get his marriage to work He became more and more isolated from the rest of humanity and this led to the possibility of suicide. From this experience came the novel Steppenwolf where the author expressed his feelings of loneliness and also saw his self as being an outsider like the wolf who wanders the grassy plains of the European steppes.

In the novel, Harry Haller - the "Steppenwolf" of the title - has left an unfinished manuscript in a boardinghouse. The nephew of the landlady discovers the manuscript and decides to publish it. The first chapter of the manuscript examines the background to the tale, with the protagonist is describing his intellectual isolation as well as his disdain of what he perceives to be narrow-minded and uninformed society along with his inability connect with people. Steppenwolf however, isn't just distinct from his elitist personality as well as his belief in his dual nature: human and of a wolf. He views his inner struggle as a struggle between his inner man that is intelligent and high-minded and the wolf within him - animalistic and low. He desires to live the life of the wolf, free from the social norms and social pressures However, he's forced to lead the life of the bourgeois bachelor and, for the sake of avoiding being labeled a'schizomaniac and'schizophreniac', must hide the psychopathic part of him. In the process, the man is becoming more removed from his peers. Naturally, the feeling of isolation is good for him however, it can also be harmful and he's conscious that it could result in insaneness. However, he has some human qualities and wishes like every human being is to be loved by all beings'. The death is, naturally an option, however Harry is averse to the notion of suicide amoral.

WOLVERINE HUCINATIONS

Harry encounters a young hedonistic woman named Hermine she introduces him the indulgences of the bourgeoisie. She teaches him about physical sensations and pleasures, such as dancing and taking drugs. Harry is exposed variety of physical experiences which are created by Hermine to bring out his various personalities. In the process, Harry's devastation is reduced and he builds a deeper connection with Hermine. However, eventually within the Magic Theatre which is a place in which Harry can experience the fantasy worlds that are only his mind - he commits murder to her , while thinking of himself as an Wolf.

In the 1960s' final years there was no bookcase for hippies complete without Steppenwolf The tale - partially autobiography, and partly fantasy - captures a variety of essential elements of hipster culture in the sixties. makeup, including sex, drugs and Buddhism. This was particularly true of the section on the "magic theater," often interpreted as psychedelic and similar to the experience of the use of LSD. Steppenwolf also became an integral part of popular culture. The significant San Francisco Magic Theatre Company adopted it's name after the story, and the band Steppenwolf formed in the year 1967, by German born John Kay, enjoyed massive international success after the appropriately called track Born to Be Wild.

"The Call of the Wild and White Fang

Jack London (1903 & 1906)

At the beginning of 1900, American author Jack London published two books on dogs and their connection to the wolf within them that remain immensely well-known to this day - The call of the wild The Call of the Wild and White Fang. Both books are mirrored In The Call of the Wild the protagonist of the book is a dog who makes an escape from the comforts of home to a life in the wild in the book, while the title of the book White Fang reverses that process moving from a life as the wolfdog back to a life of a cozy home.

The WILDS CALL

Buck is an old four-year-old part St Bernard as well as a half Scottish sheepdog who lives within the Santa Clara home of Judge Miller. In the year 2000 there is gold discovered within the Canadian Yukon Territory and large dogs that are able to pull sleds, are prized. Buck is taken in this way, and suffers brutal beatings and maltreatment while the dog is transported north, where he must quickly be able to join the ranks of the sled team. He must also be able to endure the harsh environment of the Yukon however, he begins to realize the primal instinct that had been dormant in him since the years of a comfortable life. The new strength of his is able to take on his most formidable foe, Spitz, lead dog of his group in a tense fight and take over his position.

The RHYTHM OF THE PACK

Buck is taken into the care of three adventurers from the amateur group who embark in a reckless trek through the wilderness. When they arrive at a frozen stream however, they've exhausted their food supply and Buck refuses to continue. He is saved from the subsequent assault by a man called John Thornton who warns the three of the dangers of continuing on their trip. They resent him to go on, while Buck and Thornton look on as they disappear on their sleds beneath treacherous thin ice. While Thornton is searching for the gold mine, Buck fills his time by exploring the wilderness, where he meets and runs alongside Wolfs. When he returns to his camp and he learns that his master was killed in the hands of Yeehat Indians. He seeks revenge against the murderers of Thornton, but having his ties to the world broken and his ties to civilization now broken, he responds to the calls of nature to join the wolves in singing "the songs that the pack sings'.

White FANG

White Fang is a three-quarters hybrid wolf-dog that was birthed in the wilderness. The dog and his mother are adopted by a few Native Americans, after one of them, Grey Beaver, recognizes White Fang's mother as Kiche which is his brother's wolfdog. He names the puppy White Fang, but in the Indian camp life is not easy for the dog's young age. The dogs in the camp are hostile to him, and he discovers that to live it is necessary to be more superior than them in all ways. To achieve this He transforms himself into a fierce and unstoppable combatant.

DOG-FIGHTING

At five years old, the boy is sold for one bottle of whiskey by an animal-fighter, and starts an enviable career as an athlete. At one point, it appears like he's been beaten when he's pitted against a fierce bulldog. When it appears that his chances of being killed by his adversary but he is saved by a gold prospector who is just starting out, Weedon Scott. White Fang returns to California with Scott however, he is forced to fight another battle after the man he kills is trying to take down his master, who has become a judge. The ladies of the estate where he lives affectionately call him "The Blessed Wolf because of this and the story ends with the once free-spirited White Fang lying in the sunshine on the beach in Santa Clara, the pups that he's fathered together with his dog Collie enjoying a good time with the wolf.

www.ingramcontent.com/pod-product-compliance
Lightning Source LLC
Chambersburg PA
CBHW060332030426
42336CB00011B/1305